What people are saying about The Divine Spark

This book is a volume of testimonies of God's extravagant welcome and relentless hospitality.

– Bishop Yvette Flunder, Oakland, California
Presiding Bishop, The Fellowship of Affirming Ministries
Founding Pastor, City of Refuge Church, United Church of Christ

Thirty years ago I began advocating for the acceptance of LGBTQ persons in the church. The going was tough. I could never have dreamed that a book like The Divine Spark *would appear this soon. Why did it happen? In large part because of the uncommon courage of brothers and sisters like those who contributed to this fine book. Thank you!*

– Herbert W. Chilstrom
First presiding bishop of the ELCA

Most of us hope to live an authentic life. The authors courageously describe the discovery and persistence required to strive for leading that authentic life. We are so grateful for their generous teaching.

– Mike Miller and Mary Trettin
Mike serves as President of Northland College, Ashland, Wisconsin
Both are members of Messiah Lutheran Church

This collection of stories beautifully illustrates the power of radical truth-telling and vulnerability as tools to foster change and understanding in community. Leonard Cohen wrote in his song Anthem, "There is a crack, a crack in everything / That's how the light gets in." These storytellers have embraced their authentic selves (cracks and all) and have become beacons of light in a world that desperately needs illumination.

– Mary Dougherty
Mother, Photographer, and Author
Creator of the Words for Water project
Co-founder of FarmsNotFactoriesWI.org

The Divine Spark *is a good read for anyone wondering where LGBTQ stories fit in God's story.*

- Rev. Anita C. Hill
Former pastor at Reformation Lutheran Church, St. Paul, Minnesota, and subject of the documentary film, "This Obedience."

As members of contributor Brian Henning's family of faith, we are so proud of him and so grateful to have experienced his public witness to the person God created him to be. At the same time, we lament that similar stories and experiences of exclusion and prejudice continue to play out, even in our ELCA congregations. In fellowship we add our voices to Brian's appeal for open conversation, vulnerable expressions of faith, and prayerful reconciliation so everyone might experience "thirty-seconds plus" of God's divine applause, grace, and love.

- Rev. Scott Searl
Pastor, Shepherd of the Hills Lutheran Church, Edina, Minnesota

Nancy Hanson has created a needed community resource with this collection of honest, brave, and inspirational testimonials. The people in these pages have taken an emotional leap of faith in telling their stories – and we are all the better for it.

- Julie Buckles, award-winning author of *Paddling to Winter*
Director of Communications. Northland College, Ashland, Wisconsin

The Divine Spark *is a reminder of the divinity within each of us, and the capacity we have of being fully alive. There is no experience like being oneself!*

- Paul Sturgul
Nationally recognized elder law attorney, Hurley, Wisconsin

The Divine Spark

*The first principle of Judaism
teaches us all human beings
are created in the divine image and
therefore are linked to God by the
Divine Spark within them.*

The Divine Spark

Personal Stories of LGBTQ Discovery

The Divine Spark

Published by Messiah Lutheran Church, Washburn, Wisconsin

ISBN: 978-0-9644736-1-4

First Edition

Editorial assistance by Philip J. Sorensen

Cover art by G. Scott Hanson

Book design by Copy That, Ashland, Wisconsin

Christians United Statement printed with permission from
Christians United. For details see www.christiansunitedstatement.org

This book is dedicated
to the brave and vulnerable
writers of each chapter.

Contents

The Divine Spark

Foreword

by Corinne Chilstrom

These authors form a common bond as they come to us, sharing their lives. Rejection began at a young age, simply for being born LGBTQ through no choice of their own. As teens, troubled by their own same gender attraction or gender non-conformity, they began hearing condemnation loud and clear, from both church and the broader society. Their stories pull at your heart strings as they render authentic accounts of what happened to them.

Those most hardened against LGBTQ people believe they chose their lifestyle. If only they would "confess it as sin" or "get counseling," they could be restored to a "normal, straight life."

But stay with their stories and your defenses will crumble. You will see real individual souls who have carried, often secretively and alone, heavy burdens few could have endured.

So, dear reader, we invite you to relax, take in these stories with an open heart and mind. Unmask your own core, same as these "neighbors we have from God" have unmasked themselves.

God's Spirit will move you to help the LGBTQ community, to stand up for them and advocate for their justice.

God bless you as you ponder these stories from the very essence of people who long for acceptance. May your heart receive them openly, with the doing God requires. Listen to the prophet Micah from so long ago: "What does the Lord require of you, but to do justice, and to love kindness, and to walk humbly with your God," Micah 6:8 (NRSV).

Corinne Chilstrom, retired Evangelical Lutheran Church in America (ELCA) pastor, and Herb Chilstrom, retired presiding bishop of the ELCA, both in their eighties, reside in Arizona. They are forever touched by the loss of their son Andrew, a freshman at Gustavus Adolphus College, who took his life on November 11, 1984. In 1993 Corinne wrote Andrew, You Died Too Soon, A Family Experience of Grieving and Living Again. *Herb's new book,* When A Father Loses A Son *came out in 2017.*

Introduction

Welcome. *The Divine Spark* represents a collection of stories from LGBTQ parishioners and others who answered the question: What would I say to someone of any age, but especially to a young person who is gender non-conforming, or to a young person who is starting to notice their own same-gender attraction, upon hearing the comments:

> *It is against God's will to be gay.*
> *You can pray the gay away.*
> *Men should not wear women's clothing.*
> *God wants you straight.*
> *Love the sinner, hate the sin.*
> *God hates fags.*

Messiah Lutheran council president Keith Holm, age 65, wrote the first story. He said, "Just to let you know, this is a huge step for me even after all these years."

As the articles came in, I could feel their life-giving and lifesaving nature. I offer deep gratitude to each writer for their willingness to share experiences of rejection, non-acceptance, judgment, and isolation. Thank you.

Providing the LGBTQ community and straight people a resource to promote equality serves as the principal reason for the book. Readers might also wonder what lies behind the struggle, and what they can do about it. Rev. Nate Aaseng explains the error of using the Bible to deliver such wrongful pain to LGBTQ people. Rev. Dale Chesley reflects upon his spiritual growth beginning with his first days of seminary when he struggled with women serving as pastors because the Bible forbade it. Dale's chapter lends insight and empathy for those who learn one concept, then eventually realize another, more compassionate view exists.

In the chapter, *The Next Step,* Aubrey Thonvold, Executive Director of ReconcilingWorks has listed a number of ways to collectively increase instances of acceptance, hope, and joy for gay, lesbian, bi-sexual, transgender, gender nonconforming, as well as for those who are questioning. ReconcilingWorks, a nonprofit organization, recognizes that racism, sexism, ageism, homophobia, and all other artificial distinctions seeking to advance one group's privileges and preferences over another, conspire to diminish our world and church.

The last chapter contains a description of my sabbatical project, "Forming Life-Long Faith in a Loving God." Messiah Lutheran and First Lutheran churches will send me on a sabbatical in 2018, funded by the Lilly Endowment National Clergy Renewal Program. This book comprises an integral part of the sabbatical.

Artist G. Scott Hanson designed the cover art. When asked how he came up with the image, he replied, "People are created with so much in common, yet at the same time, we are each unique." His art inspired the book's title. While reading the stories, I got the sense the writers are pleading:

Please see the love and light in me.
Please love and accept me.
God made me just as much as God made you.

Truly a divine spark lives in all of us. Let us grow in our ability to see and celebrate the Creator's work.

Love and prayers,

Rev. Nancy Hanson

Nancy serves as the pastor for Messiah Lutheran Church in Washburn, Wisconsin, and First Lutheran Church in Port Wing, Wisconsin.

Who Are You

by John Berton

Being gay is not like
being a Democrat or a Republican
it is not like
being a Christian, Muslim or Jew
it is not like
deciding to buy a BMW, VCR and condo in Lincoln Park
it is not like
voting for Ross Perot or having vanilla instead of
chocolate ice cream on that slice of pecan pie

Being gay is not a lifestyle. It is not a choice. It is like
Being Black or Asian or White or
Being 5'6" or 6'5" or
Being blue-eyed or brown-eyed

It is like having one arm, or two or
being a woman or a man or
seeing with two eyes or perhaps none

It is not something that can be changed.

Being gay is part of
BEING who you ARE

It is a discovery

The Times, They Are a-Changin'

Come mothers and fathers all over the land
Don't criticize what you can't understand
Your sons and your daughters are beyond your command
For the times they are a-changin'.

– Bob Dylan

by Keith Holm

When I was a senior in high school these lyrics were part of a four-minute speech I delivered at a state forensics meet in Wisconsin. I surprised myself by getting an A. Times were changing in the late sixties and early seventies. The war in Vietnam was coming to an end. Young people were becoming activists and love was free. Except for me.

I knew at an early age I was different from my playmates. They would look at pictures of women in bras and panties in the JC Penney catalogue. I'd look at the men's underwear models. As I grew older I finally figured out I was gay, or to use the term of the day, queer.

I knew being queer was wrong, that queers were picked on, bullied and often beat up. I wanted none of that. But I could not help who I was.

My parents took me to church on Sundays. I went to Sunday school and confirmation. It was here when I first heard being queer is a sin and queer people will be damned. Heaven was not for me. I heard it over and over in church. I heard it at home. I heard it from friends who did not know I was one of "those" people. I felt my only hope was to keep my feelings to myself and just get on with my life. My secret life.

My parents, God love them, had no clue about homosexuality. They didn't know any gay people and as good Christians no doubt my parents would have felt it their duty to change homosexuals, to pray the gay away. I wondered for a long time if I could be fixed somehow. Maybe God would make my feelings go away.

It never happened.

I concluded God did not exist. I still went to church with my family when I was a kid. I would sit there during the service hoping God would keep my secret and make sure my parents would never find out. I could not imagine how disappointed they would be if they knew their "little boy" was queer, so I continued to hide my homosexuality.

At age 29 I moved to St. Paul, Minnesota. I had a great job in a very conservative organization. I needed to keep my secret at the workplace for sure. There were no laws protecting LGBT people from discrimination in jobs and housing. No big deal, I thought. I was getting good at living and organizing my life in the closet.

One day after answering phones for a telethon in Minneapolis, I decided to walk down the street and go into the Gay 90s bar. I had never been there before. I knew it as the biggest gay bar in The Cities. I was scared to death, but went in anyway. I sat at one of the bars and ordered a drink. A diverse crowd packed the place. Men of all ages and sizes. When I emptied my glass, the bartender brought me another drink and said, "It's on that guy over there." He pointed across the bar. Oh, no. Now what? Who sent the drink? I didn't know what to do.

I remembered my manners and called the bartender over. I asked him to send a drink to the person who had bought one for me. The bartender made a drink, walked to the other side of the bar, and put it down in front of a young, incredibly handsome man. I about fell off my stool. The rest, as they say, is history.

Paul and I spent the evening together. I never believed in love at first sight, but it happened to us that night. He was 21. I was 31. For the very first time, I felt love. Real love. It felt great. We were incredibly happy.

We moved in together about a month later. Life was good.

What am I going to do about my family? I told myself I would never come out to my family unless or until I met someone I wanted to spend the rest of my life with. I knew they would go crazy. I would be kicked out of the family, taken out of the will, and would never see them again. But I was prepared for it. I met the man I wanted to spend the rest of my life with.

Mom and Dad came to visit in St. Paul fairly often. Paul was introduced as my "roommate." They bought it for a while.

The first New Year's Eve they spent with us, we put a cot in the master bedroom so Mom and Dad could stay in Paul's room. After dinner Paul started clearing the table and cleaning the kitchen. Mom offered to help, but Paul said no. He wanted her to relax and enjoy the evening. For the next year we visited Mom and Dad up north at the cottage. It was fine. We had separate beds.

The next New Year's Eve, Mom and Dad were back in St. Paul. We had a great dinner. When we finished, Paul started doing his thing, his thing being the kitchen. He hated it when someone offered to help clean the kitchen, because no one could do it as well as he could. Mom again offered to help, and Paul said, "No, thank you." She picked up some dishes and headed to the kitchen anyway. He thanked mom, but escorted her to the family room. They went home the next day. Whew, we thought. We pulled it off again.

A few days later my sister Barb called. She told me mom and dad asked her if we were gay. Nobody else would be so fussy about his kitchen. Paul must be gay! My sister had known for years I was gay, but she always kept my secret. Barb wanted to know what to tell them. I told her to go ahead and tell them.

The next morning the call came.

"Are you gay?"

Long pause.

"Yes," I said.

As expected, all of the horrible things I thought would happen, or would be said, did happen and were said.

My mom thought the devil had taken up residence in my house.

I was in my car driving to a meeting, so I pulled off the freeway into a parking lot and listened to them rant and rave for fifteen minutes.

We finally said "good-bye." I knew it would be for life. I cried my eyes out, turned the car around, and went home to my partner, my rock. He had a horrible coming out experience with his family a

4

few years earlier, so he knew what I was feeling and what I was going though.

"We will get through this," he said.

And we did.

About six months later Mom and Dad finally called and asked if they could come up for the weekend. Their words stunned me. We hadn't spoken a word since that fateful phone call.

We all spent the evening together having dinner and watching TV. The first night they slept in their camper in the driveway. The next day the four of us went sightseeing and hit the supermarket sample tables, which my dad loved. That evening mom asked if they could spend the night in the freshly named guest room. It was the beginning of a new relationship for our family.

Over the years Paul and I always felt they liked him more than me. Mom loved how he took such good care of me. In fact the whole conservative, God fearing family became quite fond of Paul. They loved him and loved that the two of us were together.

This book is about helping LGBTQ people know they remain beloved children of God. I struggled with such a notion for a long time. I could not get the words of my childhood pastor out of my head, him preaching heaven was not for me, nor for us. But how could that be? I did not believe in God, yet thought God must exist because how else could I explain my great fortune to have such a wonderful man as Paul in my life? I thought it might be a good idea to start working on exploring our spiritual life together. We tried a couple churches. One was too gay for us. The others we tried felt unwelcoming. We gave up.

About five years after we met, Paul started having some health issues so we finally decided to get the AIDS test. We would go together. No one wanted to get tested because in those days you could lose your job, housing, insurance, nearly everything. But I said we needed to do it.

Paul's test came back positive. I was negative.

For the next four years we rode the medical roller coaster of living with AIDS. Paul was in and out of the hospital. We lived by the numbers. T cell counts. Blood counts. There was only one drug available at the time. AZT became our greatest hope. AIDS finally obliterated Paul's immune system and he developed liver and throat cancer. On the 3rd of March, 1993 at 12:45 a.m., Paul's battle came to an end.

Paul passed away at home, his mom and I by his side. There was no sound. He simply stopped breathing. I knew this day would come and thought I would be ready for it. I was not. My heart was broken. My life partner gone. It scared me to think what would happen next. Would we ever be together again? Does God exist? Is heaven real? How could God let this happen?

We sat there in silence. I could hear the words of my confirmation pastor in my head. Queer people will be damned. I felt sick to my stomach.

That's when it happened. There were no words spoken. No vision or beam of light. A feeling came over me unlike anything I had ever felt. I suddenly felt warm inside. I felt like I had invisible arms around me, holding me close. I felt safe. I felt love unlike any love I had ever felt before. I will never forget it as long as I live. The feeling was indescribable. Then it was gone.

Later that day, I asked Paul's mother if she felt anything shortly after Paul passed. She described exactly the same feeling.

That night I became a believer. God touched my soul and

my heart. God let me know Paul was with Him and we would be together again. He let me know Paul was loved. He let me know I was loved. And His love was unconditional. I received an amazing gift. God's love is for everyone. It doesn't make any difference if you are gay, straight, transgender or anything on the spectrum. God took away my fear of death that night. When my time comes I will not be afraid. I will look forward to meeting God and reuniting with my partner and family and friends who have gone before me. They wait for me. I know it.

A couple months after Paul passed, I spent the weekend with my parents. As we drove to the grocery store, Mom asked me how I was doing. Then she said, "There will never be anyone like Paul. Nobody will ever take care of you like he did." These words were coming from the woman who called him the "devil" years earlier.

She went into the store leaving Dad and me in the car. Dad started to cry.

"What's wrong?" I asked.

Dad said, "I am so very sorry I wasn't there for you and made you hide your life from us."

It astonished me to hear these words from my parents. God performed a miracle with my family. It's what God does. God can perform one for you too.

It has been quite a ride. I am now 65 years old. After Paul passed, I dated from time to time. I met lots of interesting people, but none came close to him. I am still single, although Pastor Nancy keeps trying to set me up. Life is good. I moved to Washburn, Wisconsin and joined Messiah Lutheran Church. I was a little worried about being out in such a small community. As it happened, I didn't need to worry at all.

When the church considered adopting a policy allowing the pastor to marry same-gender couples, even before gay marriage became the law of the land, one member of our committee did not like the idea. He knew me from church, but did not know I was gay. During the course of discussion, I let the committee know the importance of the policy to me and to my fellow LGBT members of the community. It was essential for our church to welcome everyone and for LGBT people to feel safe in our church and community. I had outed myself to the committee, specifically, to Clayton.

At first, my friend Clayton referred to gays as "those people" during the meetings. He did not intend to be derogatory. I wondered if perhaps I was the first gay person he knew. Nonetheless, the recommendation to approve a gay marriage policy passed unanimously, largely because of Clayton's support.

One Sunday after church my new friend Clayton asked whether I would give him a ride downtown. Before he got out of the car, he asked me if I liked country music and if I liked a drink at happy hour. I told him I liked both. He told me I should stop over sometime. "Keith, you will always be welcome in my home."

It was an amazing moment. I am so glad we shared it together.

Come mothers and fathers all over the land
Don't criticize what you can't understand
Your sons and your daughters are beyond your command
For the times they are a-changin'.

As I think back on Dylan's lyrics and reflect on my personal growth as a gay man and my personal growth with God, I would have to agree that indeed the times, they are a-changin'.

When I was young no support groups, hot lines, or LGBTQ organizations existed. No PFLAG. No gay friendly congregations. We have come a long way. But we have a long way to go. If you are a young person struggling with your identity, don't give up. My story and countless others' prove how much goodness endures in the world and how people can change.

You deserve to live your life as you, and to love whom you want to love. You will run into people who won't like you very much. You will hear people who have "SBI" (Selective Biblical Interpretationitis). They will tell you being gay is a sin. Pay no attention to them. God's love is for everyone. Dylan's words still ring true. People are changing. People are becoming more and more understanding and accepting. I can say without hesitation or reservation God loves us just as we are.

Be strong!

Keith Holm, 2016-2017 Messiah Lutheran Church Council President, retired to Washburn, Wisconsin after a 29 year career as the chief executive officer of the St. Paul Area Association of Realtors.

The Divine Spark

Two-Spirited = Androgynous

*We fell in love with a person, not a gender
or an ideology, and certainly not a label.*

– Ellen Hart

by Dianne M. Heapy

I have walked as a two-spirited, androgynous person throughout my life. I did not know those terms when I was young. My life has been a spiritual journey with times of pain. Yet today I walk in contentment with the very essence and totality as a two-spirited person.

Spiritual life and faith have been the most important parts of my life since early childhood. Writing this brief autobiography has been emotionally difficult. I am grateful, however, for the opportunity to provide it for others.

"What is the purpose of this story?" Sharing my life experience might save one life, as my life was saved by my high school coach and gymnastics teacher. I was taught the only right way to be, according to society and the church community, was heterosexual. All other ways were a mistake or a sin.

During early childhood I experienced a sense of belonging with my family, and when in school and church. I eventually came to believe I did not belong – anywhere. Now I know I do belong and those teachings were wrong. I was misled.

I am okay just as I am, a two-spirited person. I was born perfectly unique, same as you, same as everyone, just as we are.

My early years filled me with happiness. I lived in Royal Oak, Michigan, a Detroit suburb, surrounded by cousins, aunts and uncles, and my grandparents. We were second generation German Americans with a Cherokee Indian great-great grandmother. I spent a lot of time with my Grandma Bauer. I remember us laughing about the old car she drove as we went places together. She liked the song "Blue Moon." I attended a Missouri Synod Lutheran parochial school during my 2nd and 3rd grade years. Church was important in our family life.

I envied my brother when he received a train set for Christmas one year. I yearned for such a wonderful toy. Instead, I got dolls because I was a girl. But, I did not like the girl toys. I did love climbing trees and being outdoors.

At eight years of age my life changed forever. My family moved to a small, southern Ohio, retired, farming town near the Bible belt. African Americans and other minorities were legally banned from the streets and sidewalks after sundown. The town was steeped in old money and an unspoken hierarchy of social class. Society viewed my family as lower middle class.

I began fourth grade in a segregated public school. Only white children attended. All students in each grade were divided into classes based on their grade point average, except for the isolated mentally disabled. I spoke differently because of my northern roots in Michigan. I had difficulty understanding my teacher because of her more southern, Kentucky accent.

I spent my weekends and summer days hiking the trails and levees and fishing the streams by the Miami River. I experienced an emotional and spiritual closeness with the trees, rocks, animals, earth, and sky. I purchased flowers, such as morning glories, and planted them in our small backyard. I liked mowing the lawn, biking, and exploring places such as the vacant old house near the housing development. Many Indian tribes had once lived in Ohio and I enjoyed reading about Indian life because the Native Americans honored all of creation and their spirituality fascinated me. Life during the summers felt good. I dreaded the end of summer and the return to school.

I have fragmented memories of the years in public school. I experienced severe bullying, name-calling, and ridicule. Other students did not include or accept me.

By high school, though a star athlete, I was suicidal. I attempted to end my life by slitting my wrists. I craved death.

My coach spent many hours talking with me when I did not have the words or comprehension of what made my life so awful. Even though I could not identify or express the thoughts and feelings of why I wanted to die, she listened to me. She compassionately talked with me about many things, including God's love for me, and that I existed as a unique, special person.

I finally met a friend. She became my girlfriend during my sophomore year of high school. We spent much of our time together, even though we lived a distance from each other. We had a physical relationship and I loved her. While I felt loved and accepted by her, I nevertheless continued to struggle with loving and accepting myself.

So I read the Bible, especially Romans. I listened to the pastor and heard my mother say things like, "If you just dressed and acted more like a girl, boys would be interested in you." I felt condemned by the Apostle Paul's writings. I kept trying to fit in and be accepted by anyone as their friend, and accepted and loved by my parents. Most of all I wanted to feel welcomed and loved by the church people, the pastor, and Jesus, who supposedly loved me because "the Bible told me so."

I graduated from high school refusing to recognize God loved me, but I knew my girlfriend loved me. We discussed how we could do life together forever. After our high school graduation, we took separate paths. My girlfriend attended a school of nursing in Ohio and I entered a Deaconess program at a Lutheran college in Minnesota. At Christmas that year my girlfriend told me her mother had found a letter she had written to me. Her mother discussed with her the awfulness and shamefulness of our homosexual relationship. My girlfriend ended the relationship by saying she had a boyfriend and would never see me again.

The following school year I met with a college chaplain and confessed my same sex relationship. He wanted me to leave the college immediately. He said I represented a threat to other women in the dorms. Eventually I left the school feeling unloved by God, unforgiven by God and the chaplain, and rejected not only by others, but also by Jesus. The childhood song says, "Jesus, loves me, this I know." I asked myself, "Where is this Jesus?"

I did not know who I was. I did not know where I belonged, and I could not understand why I felt so different from other women. I wanted to be anyone but me.

I kept trying to reconnect with the God of my childhood – the joy of family, the love and joy I experienced with God's people. I began attending an Episcopal Church while holding down a job at a large city bank, and also partying and "running with" the Dayton, Ohio chapter of The Outlaws, a motorcycle gang. It was the '60s and I used drugs, drank hard alcohol, and partied when I wasn't working.

I did not want to feel or think. Mainly, I did not want to be me.

"God, why did you create me this way, a woman who is different, considered damaged, sinful, and doesn't belong anywhere?" I asked.

My church said I could be released only through the transforming power of Jesus. To be free I simply needed to deal with the sin of homosexuality. Confess and repent. I could become "truly a new creature in Christ." Yet I had tried confessing, I tried repenting, and I felt only rejection by God even more than before.

What I did not know, but can see clearly now, was that God, Sacred Spirit, has always been with me. Sacred Spirit expressed love and acceptance to me through the times of understanding and discussions of Jesus's love by my high school coach. Sacred Spirit kept me safe during the years with the Outlaws while using drugs and alcohol. Sacred Spirit protected me during an attempted sexual assault while babysitting during my teen years. Spirit guided me with words, gentleness, and love given by a faithful community. Above all, the Sacred Presence gave me "aha" moments when I would see and experience clearly as God, the Sacred Spirit, spoke to me.

Later in life a two-spirited Ojibwe woman became my life partner. I learned from her that I am also two-spirited which explains why the spiritual and healing events have always been so important to me. In Native American culture many two-spirited people are healers, visionaries, dreamers, and keepers of the traditions. My sexuality has been only part of my life journey. My spiritual walk with Great Spirit/God represents the walk, the journey. It is because of Great Spirit, the God and Goddess of all creation, I am alive today.

Years ago I asked my partner for a copy of *Rolling Thunder* for my birthday. I received a copy of it with a card inscribed,

You said you would like a copy of this book for your very own. Here it is. It is your very own with all my love. And may the Spirit of Rolling Thunder be with you always. You, your spirit, is truly Indian. Giving you this book as a birthday gift is my pleasure. I love you.

Even though I have experienced pain and loss, I now am able to see love has truly blessed my life journey. In my reading of the Bible, the following bullet points illustrate what Spirit has shown me and what I would like to share with LGBTQ members growing up in Christian churches:

- God/Goddess is the totality of human sexuality as indicated by the empty seat on the Ark of the Covenant. It is not empty. God, the totality of all sexuality, sits upon it.

- I am, and you are, created in the image of God, the Goddess, Great Spirit. We are all descendants of the Sacred, thus our uniqueness is a Sacredness passed down through the ages, by our ancestors, beginning with God, Great Spirit, the Parent of all of us.

- We are loved and accepted just as Spirit created us in Sacred Spirit image – gay, lesbian, bisexual, transgender, queer. Spirit has made us and brought us into the world, just as we are. We were known "before the creation of the world," (Ephesians 1:4). "Before I formed you in the womb, I knew you," (Jeremiah 1:5).

- We were dedicated and known by Sacred Spirit before we were born, just as we came into the world at birth," (Jeremiah 1:4).

Paraphrasing Paul in his letter to the Corinthians:

The journey of knowing the very essence of who I am, I now understand as 'having seen my sexual identity clearly, me, as only an unknown reflection in a mirror in my youth. But now I see face to face the totality of me. I only knew in part as I was aging, but I now know fully, even as I have always been fully known by God as I am.'

What I did not know and had not been taught or shown by others was "I was fully known" always by a loving Father/Spirit. We were sent into the world, just as we are, just as God/Sacred Spirit made us to be in the world. And no one can take this away from us – ever.

A mental health professional, Dianne M. Heapy continues working in the community for quality of life for all people.

The Divine Spark

Here I Am:
Fourteen and Gay

by Sorley Swanson

My name is Sorley Swanstrom. I am fourteen years old and I am gay. Coming out as gay nowadays is far easier than it was when my parents were in high school. I am, fortunately, not under constant threat of physical abuse or teasing. In addition, the Internet can make it easier to come out. I, for example, exploded out of the closet with a Snapchat post and an Instagram picture. I received support from friends in the form of comments saying, "Way to own it dude!," or "So proud of you!"

But coming out did not arrive without its struggles. For a long time I questioned my sexuality. It wasn't until a girl asked me out that I finally came upon my realization. We went on one date and spent some time together. She helped me understand I was in fact gay. Yet it devastated her, and I felt completely responsible for her grief. My sadness, coupled with unrelenting teasing from people I considered friends, led to self-harm.

I was called names like "gay boy" and "fag." I was afraid to confront these people so I just laughed along. I eventually moved myself out of such a toxic environment and into a more accepting community of people who, like me, were part of the LGBTQ community. We all had our struggles, and having the close connection to similar people helped us through the hardships.

I pushed my way through the self-harm and negative feelings to find myself happy. I had a wonderful group of friends. I was far more outgoing about my sexuality even putting on some makeup here and there. I felt good.

Then came my gender confusion. I have male parts, but I never felt like a "boy." I stood about as far away from masculine as one could get. I felt comfortable wearing makeup. I thought I might look good in a dress, though I never had the chance to try one on. Of course, it went the other way as well. I did not feel like a girl, either.

I struggled with my identity quite a bit during my gender bewilderment. Yet I found my savior in the term "gender queer." I began using they/them pronouns. I took this identity change slower than before, telling only my closest friends. For whatever reason, gender remains a far more sensitive subject than sexuality.

Sorley Swanstrom is a ninth grader at Washburn High School in Washburn, Wisconsin. He enjoys French class, science, and show choir.

Arriving at Peace

by Anonymous

In all the years of my life, I don't think I have ever doubted the existence of God. I may have doubted myself. I may have wondered at an early age why I had feelings so different from all my other friends. Sometimes, though, a person simply must have faith and belief in their feelings, because there is no one else around who can support and listen to you. Getting to that peace of mind for me, however, meant enduring some frightening experiences.

I grew up in such an insulated environment I did not have any names for what my attraction to men was all about. The Stonewall riots had not yet occurred and on top of that, no resources, whether community or church based, were available to me. Needless to say, a child could not have made an appointment to see a therapist without his parents being made aware of the peculiarities of that discussion.

So peace was a long time coming.

Peace certainly would not have come to our house had I voiced my concerns and questions. My parents, both devout Christians, believed in the literal translation of the Bible. It had to be the King James Version, the version that raised all good Scandinavians. My parents served as pillars of the church, filling volunteer positions, like organist, Sunday school teacher, deacon, singer, vacation Bible school instructor, counselor at summer Bible camp, and fill-in for the pastor in the pulpit when the pastor was on vacation or had been called away on short notice. It was not uncommon for one of our family or the whole family to be found at the church at least three or four times a week. In fact, everyone downright expected we would be there.

But I never felt any rebelliousness. Instead, I thrived, loving the community, basking in the social and spiritual aspects of the church. Living the love. There was a lot of love in our family. We deeply cared for each other on a spiritual, ethical, and daily level. Neighbor helped neighbor. The church in town where we worshiped stood as an important cog in the cultural wheel of our small community. I grew up loving – loving my family, loving God. We never wanted for anything. Life felt wonderful in our little corner of the world.

Not until the 70s brought cultural strides for the civil rights of different groups of people did things start happening for me. I graduated from high school in the early 70s, ready to set foot in the world. I still had security and support from my family, much like all good people who receive their diploma. They say goodbye to their alma mater. They say goodbye to various teachers who schooled them in the tried and true subjects of science, mathematics, literature, history, and many other topics of training to gird them, making them ready to succeed in society. The most important person in my life at that turning point became me. I knew Mom and Dad would always be there, but I had to take responsibility for myself. This became apparent as I struck out on my own.

Following two years of community college, I enrolled at a university. No one in my family had ever attended an institution of higher learning. I became the first. All during this time I was growing, learning about society, community, sexualities, cultures; in other words, the world around me.

By this time I knew what to call myself, a homosexual, or in more common terms, a gay person. I was attracted to men. Sometimes it was hard to miss seeing people like me on the news. Most always, stories about gays and lesbians had a negative slant. A common factor tied all the stories and news events together; the words, "They chose that lifestyle, so let it be so."

Lest you think like a lot of folk who believe I chose my sexual orientation, who believe I decided I liked men and it represented a purely sinful choice, such is not the case. Because of my close relationship with God – that is to say, as close as a humble follower can be – I prayed to God often, wondering why I was who I was.

Early on, I prayed. I prayed as a boy who could not understand why he could be someone whose very nature would disturb his parents. I prayed asking, "What is the reason for me being the way I am?" Sometimes nightmares filled my head as I thought about why would I want to even choose such a sexuality if my parents had such negative news of it?

As I came into my adulthood, my prayers wondered, "How could I be made into an instrument of peace?"

I was in my twenties when on Memorial Day weekend during an innocent shopping trip to a bigger town, I found all the stores had closed earlier than expected. What to do: go home and spend the evening with Mom and Dad watching television, or enter that gay bar in the downtown area I had heard about? Countless times around the block I went. What would I find inside if I went through those doors?

And then I found myself inside. It was an incredible place. Bright colors, loud music, and more people than I had ever expected. So I was not alone after all. Others like me existed. These people did not appear sad or forlorn, nursing their drinks at a long, lifeless bar as the bartender looked on. No, these people were enjoying themselves, visiting, telling jokes, complimenting each other, offering to help each other out. In other words, a group of people at a favorite watering hole, just like any other.

By the end of the evening I was going home with a young guy I found very pleasant. And by the end of the summer I met a person whom I would deem my lover, someone whom I would love forever and move in with immediately.

Well, romance is fleeting and so neither of the relationships worked out. The guy I moved in with even proceeded to call me a hypocrite for having an intimate relationship with him and then going to church each Sunday.

Needless to say, loving coupling did not last more than several months after which I spent another few months extricating myself from the living arrangement.

When I looked back at my life, I felt I had to come to grips with my sexuality through my personal faith in God. I did not have a family that supported me. More often than not the people I met, although ethically fine, upstanding gentlemen and ladies, were not schooled in the Bible or in religion in general, possibly because they had been ostracized by the very people who should have exemplified love and kindness.

Often I had partners who did not even accept I was religious.

After all of the above, and now into what people who are my age would call their "senior years," I have tried to stay true to myself and to who I am. I admit I have probably not lived the best example of what a gay man should do in his life. I have made some bad decisions and I ask for forgiveness almost hourly. At the same time, I constantly thank God for the riches He has given me. Richness of family, friends, and community, richness of a life lived well and full. I am eternally thankful for the love and joy and the promises He has given me. Such standards guide my life.

This peace stills my soul.

Today I live my life purposefully. I have a partner. We have been together a number of years. I thank God for him. I try to live as a Christ-like example to him and to all my friends. I trust that someday God will say, "Time for you to come home, son," and I will be with God forever.

God will ask if I have loved Him well and whether I have loved my neighbor as myself. I will answer, "Yes, I have earnestly tried to care for those who hurt, feed those who are hungry, and minister to those who are lonely."

Then I will take a deep breath and say, "I've had good and bad days. I've been a hypocrite and a liar. But I believe in You and trust in Your goodness and mercy."

I will hear God say, "I know." Then I will look forward to His words, "Well done, my good and faithful servant."

And I will enter into glory with God forever.

The author chooses to remain anonymous.

The Divine Spark

Thirty Seconds Plus

by Brian Henning

My conflict with my sexuality began when I was in middle school in Pennsylvania. As a bigger kid who struggled with his weight and body image, I justified my thoughts and feelings as typical jealousy of my male classmates confident in their physiques. As I continued through high school and college, however, I began to realize my justification consisted of simply that – rationalization and avoidance. Yet, at the same time, I also got bullied through my school years for "acting gay." I came to believe I could not be gay, because then I would be proving the bullies right after so many years of denying it.

Once I began my seminary journey, I had a feeling I could no longer repress my identity. I cannot explain my awareness in words. I do know staying in the closet could not last as an option. After many sleepless nights, hours of reflection, and profuse prayers for clarity, I finally made the decision to come out to my family, friends, and colleagues. Every single person I told greeted my coming out with love and support. Joy and immense gratitude filled my senses.

Yet it also became clear the same love and support felt in coming out was not a universal response. I had heard the stories of hate and rejection toward others in the LGBTQ+ community, but that came from other places and from people whom we would stereotype as anti-LGBTQ+.

When I began the process for an internship site as part of my seminary journey, the potential supervisors with whom I interviewed met me with hesitation. Two congregations explicitly told me I would not be welcome in their community. I found opaqueness from the rest. Too often I received the response that, while most people would accept having an openly gay intern, some would oppose it vocally. Further, I often heard that the conversation was frankly too difficult to have so they avoided it altogether.

Not until a month after the internship assignments came out, however, did I feel the true complacency and discrimination of the Church. The church hierarchy informed me no internship site existed for me because the Contextual Education department could not find a congregation willing to welcome me into their community. I was crushed. I began questioning everything: my call, my identity, and even my belief in a loving, grace filled God.

By the love and support of my family, friends, and colleagues, I pushed on in my studies. I grieved, lamented, wrote our Presiding Bishop, and began talking. I talked to pastors, professors, and friends. I became aware of the deep, anti-Lutheran, anti-Reformation, anti-Gospel theology of scarcity and smugness throughout our church. But most importantly, I learned God had called me to be a voice in the wilderness – to challenge authority in our culture and proclaim the Gospel message of love and welcome for all.

I got rejected for an internship the same semester I learned about a theological concept called perichoresis. It holds one must be their true, authentic self in order to have a relationship with another. Specifically, we, as children of God, must act as our whole, God-created selves in order to live in a pure relationship with God and with others. What an utterly transformative thought. It helped me see the "box" which others had forced me into and stood inherently against the person God wants me to be.

Therefore, after even more conversation and prayer, I decided to take the next step in claiming my identity. I presently work as the Children's Ministry Coordinator for a congregation in Edina, MN called Shepherd of the Hills Lutheran. The staff and council president knew of my sexuality, but we never made a big statement about it. I never thought it relevant and so I never told anyone. Nonetheless, nondisclosure can become a part of living in the closet. I did not know how someone might react if I told them, or how the people they might tell would respond. So I said nothing.

After the events of the internship assignment process, though, I knew remaining in the closet in any sense of the idea could no longer serve as a viable option. So on Pentecost of 2017 at the end of worship, I told my story to everyone present in the sanctuary.

It was indeed terrifying, but also unbelievably freeing. I did not, however, expect the reaction. I figured some to be affirming, others to be vehemently against, and most to not really care. Instead, I received a thirty-second plus standing ovation. Not one person in the sanctuary remained seated.

After worship, the congregation further greeted me with hugs, kind words, concern for my well-being, and a sense of urgency to become a force and a voice of change. I felt awed.

Now I am well removed from the emotional pain of the above series of events. I am working on finding a new internship site for next year and am transforming into my new understanding of my calling. My ministry will not look like the traditional model of how people think of a pastor, and that is okay. In fact, it is a good thing. The church remains a unique place filled with unique people. This is not something to be ashamed of, but celebrated.

Some people who claim they are the church have hurt me. But they are not the church. The people who have restored me represent God's true church. I felt the love and grace of God through the love and grace of those who supported me. This epitomizes true faith and what God intends for us. God wants us to be whom God created us to be – special, extraordinary and in God's image.

God celebrates every aspect of our personhood. Anyone who claims discrimination justified by biblical interpretation needs to reread their Bible. God's story exemplifies deep, compassionate love for the children God created – all of them. Simply put, we are created in God's image and no one can ever take that away from us.

The church members who gave Brian Henning the standing ovation offered Brian his internship experience and future call. He has thrived at Shepherd of the Hills Lutheran Church in Edina, Minnesota.

I Feel Like a Woman

by Carri Hoagland

Mine has been an interesting journey to say the least. I was born in Texas, the Lone Star state, as Clifford Eric Hoagland. I was baptized Presbyterian and attended Sunday school and church. I did not have much choice since my mother served as organist. I remember sitting in the front row with a coloring book, subjected to my mother's scorn if I or my sisters did anything wrong.

After moving from Texas to Port Wing, Wisconsin when I was in middle school, my parents took me to the Lutheran church to attend Sunday school.

I remember my teacher and how we read the King James Version. None of it made sense. Of course my involuntary attendance didn't help matters. Memorization was important, even if we did not understand what the words meant.

Confirmation was pretty much the same. We had to do it, so all of us went. Since all my friends also attended, the group spirit helped us get through the entire ordeal.

After confirmation, church became the last thing on my mind. I was a young buck, carefree, and life was good. I never went to church except for a funeral or wedding.

In my early thirties I met the most wonderful and beautiful girl in the world. She grew up attending church, so we continued the tradition. We had three daughters, all of whom were baptized. Pastor Joe presided at two of our daughters' weddings on the shore of Lake Superior. We went to young couples gatherings and retreats and I became more interested in the way of the Lord and how God affected our lives. I realized the church leaned conservative, but at the time, it did not make much difference to me. Our children enjoyed Sunday school, vacation Bible school and other church activities.

Eventually a number of folks left the church because of infighting. My family also left. A couple friends attended a very conservative church a little distance away and we started going there. The Covenant Church had a large couples group. We remained very active. I helped in the construction of an addition because of the growing attendance.

As things went along, my life was going through monumental changes. After a lot of therapy, I began to comprehend I was transgendered. I also was retiring after twenty years of teaching at a technical college.

Because of my gender change, my wife and I separated. It certainly put a lot on my plate. My wife and I still love each other, not romantically or sexually, but as very good friends. We have three daughters and we saw no need to be hateful and bitter. My wife could not envision a relationship with a female.

While undergoing the change, my wife and I asked to speak to the pastor of our church. I should have known what might happen. I remember he had preached open hatred and denial against LGBT people.

We met one afternoon and told him of my major transformation. He never questioned or asked anything, but opened up the Bible to Deuteronomy 22:5 which basically says, "Men shall not wear women's clothes and women shall not wear men's clothes."

He closed the book and said I would not be accepted in the church. (He also told my wife later if I did appear, then he would have the ushers take me out.) As we left the church that afternoon while walking to the car, I crackled to my wife, "So much for the children's song 'Jesus Loves Me This I Know.'"

Needless to say, I never went back to the church and neither did my wife, even after we separated.

As things became tougher and more stressful, I needed to worship and be with the Lord. All my gender changes were going on during the last few months of my employment prior to retiring. One of the financial people at the college where I taught was a good friend and openly gay. Peter was one of the few folks with whom I secretly opened up, and he said, "Why don't you come to my church?" He said it was open and affirming. At the time I did not know what that meant, but I thought about it a little and one Sunday I went. I was still living a dual life, teaching as a male chauvinist pig during the week, and then on Sunday mornings sneaking out of my small town as a female. Talk about a nerve-wracking life.

I showed up and sat in the back pew near the door with an escape plan. Get up, left turn, out the door, and I would be free. I sat there. A nice elderly lady later known to me as Gertrude Jacobson, put her hand on my shoulder and said, "We are so glad you came."

That made all the difference. I started attending and eventually became an official member. I have done everything imaginable. I have cooked, presided over Bible studies, led the women's retreat, served on all the committees possible, sat on the director's board, and now I am teaching Sunday school. I was totally accepted at a time when I needed it the most, the time during my transition. The church is my family.

The women of the church threw me a shower prior to my trip to Thailand for sexual reassignment surgery. It meant the world to me. They traveled with me to the airport to see me off. Most memorably, my friend Tiss had the music changed at the Duluth airport as we walked in at 5:30 in the morning. It went from nice, quiet tunes to Shania Twain singing, "I Feel Like a Woman." Tiss just giggled.

All of it was wonderful, but more importantly, I learned a whole different level of acceptance and love for God. No longer was I told what I had to believe. No longer was I told what I had to do to please my Higher Power. I did not have to fear God any longer. I got to understand God as I understood God.

God is the one who stands beside me and guides me. God reprimands me and then encourages me. I am not a perfect Christian by any means. I use four letter words. I have bad thoughts. I do things which I realize later I should not have said or thought about in such a way.

I now live knowing I will make mistakes, but with God's help I can correct them and make apologies. God stands now as my loving friend with whom I can have a quiet talk. God does not condemn me. God does not scare me. Sometimes I don't like what I am led to do because of the difficulty. I wonder where it all will lead.

I will end this chapter with perhaps my favorite memory. I recall waking up in the ICU from my surgery in Thailand. I am not one who has ever had a divine vision, for goodness sakes. But that night I remember looking down a foggy road not knowing what was at the end or how I would traverse it. Suddenly the road went on forever with no fog under a clear, blue sky. There stood a person in a white robe holding my hand. Not a word was said and I never looked at him, or her. It still brings tears even as I write this. I now know as long as I bring the Lord with me, anything is possible.

I think of a statement in our church. "We are pilgrims on a journey together seeking God's will on earth through study, discernment, and service. Amen."

Amen.

Carri Hoagland, retired auto mechanics instructor, pilot and parent, is active at Pilgrim United Church of Christ in Duluth, Minnesota. She travels around the United States giving talks on transgender issues.

The Divine Spark

Acceptance

by Anonymous

I call my father a fundamentalist, evangelical atheist. My partner's father was a fundamentalist, evangelical Lutheran. Each was sincere and earnest in his position on existence, confident of his research into the basis of what he held to be true. Each thought his position stood as the only possible one. Those who did not agree needed to be convinced to change, converted.

In 1991, when I let my parents know my interests lay in men and not women, my mother was not completely pleased but very accepting. I think she wanted me to have kids. My macho father from whom I expected the worst commented, "Well, you're still the same Yann, aren't you?" What more could anyone want from anyone else on that subject?

To this day I get tears in my eyes when I think of my father's comment. Years later, after my father had met my partner and long before marriage became legal, he commented to me one morning, "If you were married, Adam would be my son-in-law." Again, I get tears in my eyes just thinking of that remark. It stands as one of the most accepting moments I've ever had on coming out. My father had completely accepted Adam as my partner.

My partner's rather large family consists mostly of funda-mentalist, evangelical Christians of various denominations. His father once took my hand, stared into my eyes, and asked if I had taken Jesus as my personal savior. A few members of my partner's family (mostly, but not only, the younger set) have completely accepted and honored our relationship. Many others in the family have been very unaccepting. The outward displays of hostility toward my partner and me, mostly me, have stopped, but I suspect the internal sympathies remain not very different from where they stood at the beginning. I believe if I vanished from my partner's life, a great relief would settle among many in his family.

I had let my father know Adam was devout, comfortable, and happy in his Lutheran beliefs and asked him to lay off the conversion attempts. He did.

From what I know of Christianity, Jesus welcomed, honored, accepted everyone. Not so for most 'Christians' I have met. I always wonder what goes through the minds of each congregation member as the pastor preaches acceptance of people regardless of their skin color, their sexual orientation, their gender, their financial position, or any of the myriad aspects of humanity. Are they listening? Is their brain going 'not me' as she speaks? Are they busy reviewing their Netflix choices for the evening? They care greatly if they perceive disrespect of their religion on TV, in movies, in speeches, in print, but they do not seem to understand the relationship between religious doctrine and their life as they live it.

It is ironic to me that my atheist father was more able to find it within himself to accept a relationship between his son and another man than his Christian counterpart, my partner's father.

In 2018, due to fear for my safety, I have chosen to remain anonymous. In the USA, MY country as much as it is anyone's, because of the person I love, my financial and physical safety are in jeopardy outside certain areas of large cities. In September, 2017, in an amicus brief to my Supreme Court, the attorney general of my country advocated that businesses and governmental organizations be free to deny services to people who love someone of the same gender. How such people might be identified, stereotypes notwithstanding, is not immediately obvious. Something like the yellow stars used by Nazi Germany during the Second World War to identify Jewish people comes to mind.

The Divine Spark

Odyssey to Kindness

When you are born in a world you don't fit in; it's
because you were born to help create a new one.

— Anonymous

by Stephanie Winter

Try as I might, I have always felt like an outsider and a nonconformist, although I've managed to appear as if I fit into mainstream culture. When the above quote floated across my Facebook feed, I realized in my own small way, it's always been up to me, a small town, sixty-two-year-old lesbian/feminist/chronically ill woman who has spent so much of her life longing for and working for acceptance, to provide a space for others to feel welcomed, cared about, and embraced for whoever they are in their deepest, essential selves.

Yes, I am an idealist, a spiritual seeker, a philosopher and adventurer, an introvert, and a highly sensitive person. But labels only give you a sense of who I am; they do not reveal the inner workings of my soul. And so, I set out at a young age to begin my journey of a lifetime.

My spiritual search – for the core of who I am – began on the farm where I was raised and continued when my small, southeastern

Minnesota United Methodist church confirmed me. I was devoted
to my church in a way the rest of my family was not. It provided
friends, a community of support, and the opportunity to serve in the
choir and as a Sunday school teacher. Every bit of it helped me feel
good about myself.

In late high school I attended another church with my then
boyfriend. We met in a congregant's home to listen to tapes
translating the Bible directly from Greek and Hebrew. There I felt
studious, serious, and special. By college, though, I broke away from
the church to find something more meaningful and to explore my
identity intellectually, spiritually, emotionally, and sexually. I could
no longer rely on someone else to tell me what was sacred and how I
fit into the larger universe. I needed to find out for myself.

My father and I could not know a letter he wrote post-college
as I prepared to move in with a college boyfriend would direct
the rest of my life. Both my parents expressed concerns about my
decision to live with a man to whom I was not married. Although
a sexual revolution had begun in the 1960s, cohabitation still served
as the exception, not the norm. My father felt I had succumbed to
peer pressure. In his letter Dad urged me to "march to the beat of a
different drummer." From Henry David Thoreau's Walden:

*If a man does not keep pace with his companions, perhaps it is because
he hears a different drummer. Let him step to the music which he hears,
however measured or far away.*

Neither Dad nor I understood the way he and Mom raised me
and the unique person he encouraged me to become, in combination
with the letter he wrote, would help move me even further outside
societal norms. In 1981 I fell in love with a woman and embraced
my identity as a lesbian. It had become clear to me, even though I

had been in intimate relationships with several men, my strongest and most meaningful relationships had occurred with women. Nevertheless, I tried valiantly to fit into the confined circle of small town norms and motherly expectations: to become, first and foremost, a wife and mother. Consequently, after I reached my mid-20s and was living on my own in the Twin Cities, I also was reluctant and terrified to confront and reframe the expectations of everyone I knew, including myself.

By the late 1970s I had been volunteering for several years at Amazon, a lesbian/feminist bookstore in Minneapolis. Lesbian co-workers surrounded me and we catered to lesbian shoppers on a regular basis. My world and my reality gradually shifted and expanded. What became normal to me, however, had not become the norm for the small community of my childhood and adolescence.

I told my mother first.

Her response, "Don't ever tell your father. It will kill him."

I waited several years to write my dad a letter. As it turned out, my father, who at some earlier point had paid a short visit to Amazon bookstore with two of his older feminist sisters, was less surprised and less disappointed.

Several years later a medical diagnosis of Type 1, insulin-dependent diabetes shocked me. The world I knew shattered. My body was broken, my self-concept wounded, and my ability to be loved was destroyed. At least, that's what I thought. I felt incredible shame about my now imperfect body.

At age twenty-nine I was supposed to be healthy and vibrant. I felt alone and undesirable; thankfully, I found that wasn't the case. I will be the first to admit, however, maintaining a relationship while managing a chronic health condition has its challenges.

In the thirty-some years since my coming out as a lesbian and a person with diabetes, I can 'pass,' no problem. I don't look butch. I think I appear more androgynous. Also, you cannot 'see' my diabetes; unless you're around me when I pull out my blood testing machine or fill my insulin syringe for my early morning and pre-meal shots. I do not have the same struggles as some of my peers – gay men, butch women, and transgender people, whose appearance may not adhere to conventional norms and expectations.

I feel fairly comfortable in my own skin. Yet I occasionally find myself consciously or unconsciously evaluating how I will be accepted when I change jobs or neighborhoods, join new groups, or even sit down in my assigned seat on an airplane. I keep coming out to others over and over again about my sexuality and the diabetes, while I struggle to engage and prevail in the battle within myself for self-esteem and deservingness.

Regrettably, the human tendency to compare myself to those with more money, attractiveness, and intellect, and with better diabetes management (i.e., lower readings on their HbA1c tests) leaves me lacking. I am discovering my self-criticism only abates when I choose to accept myself and embrace my skills and abilities in addition to my flaws and failings.

Throughout my lifetime of seeking – my years of learning to live with, accept, and flourish – my identity as a lesbian and a woman with a chronic illness have influenced me more than anything. I have experienced how unhelpful it is to get judged because of my sexual preference or my physical inabilities. As a result, I have learned to open my heart and have practiced becoming less judgmental of the wide variety of differences between people of all races, cultures, sexual preferences, and abilities. I have learned the oft-forgotten truth that we are all One. I have chosen to walk upon the earth in a way modeled by my father, a farmer who revered beauty and silence, respected animals, plants, and all living creatures, and appreciated the never-ending cycles of life, death, and regeneration.

My lifetime journey has introduced me to a world of ideas and other cultures through travels in Canada, Western Europe, Scandinavia, Mexico, and Central America, as well as other states in the U.S. In my early thirties I enrolled in a 'design-it-yourself' human development graduate program to discover how to live with chronic illness by balancing mind/body/spirit/emotions. While studying human development, I attended workshops and classes on empowerment, forgiveness, attitudinal healing, and psychosynthesis. I learned Reiki, a form of energy healing; the Chinese martial art t'ai chi ch'uan; and then t'ai chi chih™, a form of moving meditation, which I also taught. These have all had a huge influence on me.

Over the years I have meditated, prayed, read the Bible, attended spiritual retreats, gone solo on my own spiritual retreats, and explored shamanism and paganism. I have searched for – and found – people, words, images, and personal experiences which have fed me emotionally, intellectually, and spiritually. Some of the most important words came from Rachel Naomi Remen, a psychologist/writer/teacher/healer who wrote, "The purpose of life is to grow in wisdom and to learn to love better." To me, that represents a huge, magnificent, and worthy goal.

In 2002 after eight years together, my lesbian partner and I moved to live in the woods north of Bayfield, Wisconsin. It was glorious for both of us to revisit the peace and tranquility of living close to the land, under the trees, and within the web of existence. She also grew up on a farm. Our 'family' now included black bear and wolves, in addition to our geese, cat, and dog. Since we both were introverts, we could not have been happier.

The sound of the wind through the leaves, the song of birds, the stamp of deer hooves, and the long nights of silence blessed us. Of course, our relationship status preceded us. A man from whom we bought firewood told us he had heard two gay guys had bought the property where we lived. We did occasionally receive subtle and not so subtle messages about our lifestyle. Word travels fast in a small town. We worked hard to find connections and gain acceptance as we built a small health and wellness business.

Since transplants from Minneapolis–St. Paul, Madison, and other cities fill northwestern Wisconsin, we connected with former metropolitan residents who shared our values and experiences. We ourselves had lived thirty plus years in the Twin Cities. The old timers, people who had grown up locally and who had chosen to raise their families here, reminded us of our younger lives spent on the farm and the benefits of small town community life. Here we lived in the best of both worlds.

Unfortunately, the stress and pressures of dealing with my declining health, property upkeep, and different values and priorities split apart our partnership. We ended our almost twenty year relationship.

Now a resident of Washburn, Wisconsin, I feel as if I have become an accepted and valued part of the community. As I've grown older, I feel less of a need to explain myself or to live according to other people's expectations. Also, as my memories fade and I gain more self-acceptance, the pain of existing as an outlier in a society and culture that pressures and cajoles us to act, dress, speak, and believe in a particular way lacks the significance it once held.

In her memoir "Marrow: A Love Story," author Elizabeth Lesser writes about her sister's dying process and their joint effort to heal their relationship:

...our own journey never ends. There is no finish line. There is always more to uncover, more to know, more to heal, more to love, more to give. Being true to oneself is a rough-and-tumble ride, full of challenges and wonders.

I am on a lifelong odyssey. It asks me to become the most loving, accepting person I possibly can by welcoming and embracing those who struggle for love and acceptance, which, truth be told, is all of us. My spiritual search and personal experiences have taught me well. I can always be kinder. I can always aim to create more peace within myself. I can always open my heart just a tiny bit wider.

Steph Winter lives near Lake Superior where she walks its shoreline, breathes in lake air, and practices t'ai chi chih™ moving meditation. She works at Washburn Public Library and is blessed with friends who understand her need for quiet and solitude.

The Divine Spark

Will You Love the You You Hide?

by Rev. Jason Clifton

It was a crisp, sunny, October afternoon in Seattle. A year earlier at the age of 23 I sold my house, a half mile down the road from my parents' home. I packed all my belongings and moved 1700 miles away to Issaquah, Washington for school. I had lived in a small town my entire life. I was excited and terrified at the same time. Little did I know I would discover what it meant to be a beloved child of God, just as I was.

That October afternoon in 2007 I was at my practicum site as part of my service learning for college credit. I volunteered at an after school program. It was close to Halloween and a couple kids wanted to paint the nails of the adults. All of us obliged. On the way home I looked at my hands and realized who I was, my whole self. It dawned on me how much I had been trying to exist as someone I was not. "I was gay."

I am not sure what about that specific act and moment brought so much clarity. But then we don't get to choose those moments.

So began the process of coming out. A process as terrifying as moving across the country, only this time I was preparing to go it alone. Several friends I met in Seattle had been disowned by their families, fired from their jobs, and abandoned by friends and the church. We felt the structures upon which we relied to build our individual and collective identities had collapsed. Those calamities shaped my expectations of what I also would experience.

Having been raised in the Evangelical Lutheran Church of America (ELCA), I was attending a small liberal arts Lutheran college. I went to college with plans to attend seminary to become a pastor. But because of my self-revelation and subsequent coming out, I figured becoming a pastor would never happen.

My experience, however, had a different aspect than others. My closest friends from high school stood by me. An interim pastor, whom I had met only twice yet trusted because my mother trusted her, helped me come out to my parents. My brother and parents felt no surprise. My church community continued to support me. Make no mistake, I had to part ways with some friends, and the relationship with my sister remains a work in progress.

Nonetheless, even though my own coming out met with kindness instead of scorn, I knew the church could do better. We can teach the church how to exercise compassion and how to offer assistance. Many of us know what it means to hide one's identity from our friends and family. We found safety in hiding the truth, even from ourselves, as well as from God.

In 2009 the ELCA voted to ordain LGBTQ ministers who were publicly out and were in relationships. A pastor friend called and said, "Well, now you can go to seminary." So I did. I went to seminary and came to know other LGBTQ clergy and seminary students through Proclaim, a ministry of Extraordinary Lutheran Ministries.

What advice can I offer? Live into the person God has created you to be. Surround yourself with a community that will support and love you for who you are. Know there will be relationships which may end and others which take great amounts of effort. Most importantly, though, know you are a beloved child of God, just as you are.

You are a gift to the church. I close with my modified words from John Bell's song, "Will You Come and Follow Me?"

Love the you you hide.
Trust in God to quell the fear inside and never be the same.
Use the faith you've found to reshape the world around.

Jason Clifton serves as pastor at Our Savior's Lutheran Church, Solon Springs, Wisconsin. He enjoys the outdoors, quilting, singing in choirs, and attending area sporting events.

The Divine Spark

My Sister, My Brother

by Niki Pohnl

I am the proud parent of three children – Caden, 22; Anthony, 19; and Caroline, 12. My oldest son Caden came out to us as transgender three years ago. It affected each person in our family differently.

I worried mightily about Caden's emotional and physical well-being during his coming out. I could not begin to understand what it was like to live his life. It got me thinking, what has it been like for his siblings? I know how I see the process, but what about Caroline, then nine years old? What has she noticed? Where has she seen change? What has she learned? Does she struggle? At times I saw my daughter reflect on how she once had a big sister, and I know she grieved that loss.

I had to write a paper for a class I took last year. My task was to interview someone who went through a traumatic event and compare it to the five senses. I chose to interview my daughter Caroline, by then age ten, one year after the transition started. I hoped it might help her recognize how far she has come through the process, how much happier her older sibling became, and how to identify the support she has around her in anticipation of another traumatic experience in her life.

From Caroline's interview:

What is it like, being a sibling of a transgender person? I have an older sister and an older brother. If you had asked me a year ago about what it was like to be a nine-year-old with two teenage siblings, then I probably would have answered with heartfelt stories about family movie night, family game night, family meals, and times I got to hang with them in their rooms – a big deal to me. Asking me the same question at age 10 is a little different story, because now my big sister is transitioning to be another brother. Put yourself in my shoes and hear what my last year has been like.

In the beginning, transition felt very sad. So sad I would not have my sister anymore. I was used to having a brother and a sister, not two brothers. I didn't go to school for two days after I found out. I just wanted to hold my teddy bear and be close to my mom and dad. Transition felt confusing. Why would she want to do this? What else in my family was going to change? Why wasn't my mom crying about this like I was? Transition felt scary. How was she going to change? What would she look like? Will she still like to hang out with me? What if I make a mistake and call him 'Andrea?' Will she be mad at me? Or will he be mad at me? I asked my mom to take down some of the pictures of me and my sister because it was a reminder of who she wasn't going to be anymore.

At the same time, transition felt comforting. Mom and Dad assured me this was the best thing for Andrea; this was what would make her happiest in her life and that's what they wanted for all their children. Transition felt calming as we prayed for her every night. We prayed God would help her make the best decision for herself, and we prayed that God would keep her safe in the process. Transition felt reassuring as I talked to the school guidance counselor about grief and began to understand what was happening to me and my family.

Transition sounds mixed up. Sometimes I hear my sibling referred to as Andrea and sometimes Caden. Sometimes I hear and say 'she' and sometimes I hear and say 'he.' Conversations sound so confusing. I hear us being so good about the change in name and pronouns, until we talk about the past and we refer to 'she' and 'Andrea,' and then our words get so mixed up again.

Transition also sounds like some friends and relatives refusing to make the name change.

Transition sounds like anger. The first few months of the testosterone shots, Caden was angry a lot. He got angry with me for leaving my dance bag on the living room floor. He got angry with me for not getting to bed exactly on time. 'No worries. It's not his problem,' Mom would say when it made me sad. Little things just made him angry.

Transition sounds like Mom saying the same thing over and over, 'We have to be patient. It's the drugs entering his system that make him this way right now. When his body gets used to the drugs he will be more pleasant to be around.'

Transition sounds like a funny voice change.

Over the past year, transition at my house looked like change. Caden's bedroom color changed from purple to white and different pictures went up on his walls. Caden's bathroom products changed. Pictures in our house began to change.

Transition looked like correction. Always correcting ourselves when we said 'she' or 'her' or 'Andrea' when we meant to say 'he,' 'his,' or 'Caden.' Actually, I am the best at the pronoun transition, more than anyone in my family.

Watching my brother transition looked like shots, drugs, and injections on a weekly basis. It looked like hairy legs, hairy armpits, and larger gauges in his ears. Transition looked like a binder, a dress shirt, and a necktie for work.

And transition smelled like Axe body wash.

Along the way, transition has felt like family support. Watching us interact like the family we always have been no matter what we are going through – highs and lows at dinner time, bonfires in the back yard, openly talking about the process.

Transition feels like school support. Mom and I talked to all of my teachers before 4th and 5th grades so they knew about our family dynamics and they knew how best to support me when I was at school.

Transition felt like summer therapy. Learning about what it all means and watching the process unfold made the transition easier for me.

Transition feels like comfort. Comfort in knowing this is what my brother wants and it makes him happy. Comfort in still getting to hang out with him once in a while, because I love that!

Now, transition feels like love and acceptance. Transition looks normal. Saying 'he' is easy for me. And one of the proudest moments for me during this transition so far was that he changed his name to Caden so his name would start with the same letter as mine. I love my brother no matter what.

...It is my hope the parents of another child, or the sibling going through a similar situation, will recognize the resilient nature of children and how they grow to become accepting, non-judgmental, and well-rounded. People told my husband and me they felt sorry for Caroline having to go through something like this at such a young age. Yet we feel blessed. Caroline sees people as people and does not judge, question, or care about their gender. Caroline has learned what it is all about. It is all about love and respect.

Niki Pohnl is the Director of Discipleship and Ministry at English Lutheran Church in La Crosse, Wisconsin and has formed a support group for parents of transgender children.

The Divine Spark

I am an Episcopalian.
I am a Priest.
I am Gay.

by Rev. Mark Ricker

First, I cannot resist the need to apologize for those in the church who have, or who continue to judge you and tell you God does not love and accept you for who you are. Whether you are gay or straight, God made us that way and I celebrate you and hope you also find love and acceptance in the pages of this book and in the many and increasing groups and churches who also can give support. I welcome you and celebrate you too. God loves you and I hope to show you specific ways to see and understand that love.

Second, I want to let you know you are going to find, in growing numbers, that God is moving in our world and in our culture to allow more and more LGBTQ folks to experience the possibility of a more normal life, as well as ways to love whom you want to love without reproach or criticism. As with many other challenges in the life of the church and in our Western culture, it has taken a long time to accept mixed race marriages, to treat people of color the same way as white folks, to allow women the same rights and positions as men, and to advance other social justice and civil rights issues. Sadly, it often seems like the church takes longer than other institutions to find the way to love and accept when faced with such differences.

Furthermore, I hope anything of what I share will help you avoid some of the difficult things I encountered as a gay Christian in a world which did not accept both loving Jesus and loving others of my own gender. Thank God the scenario is changing.

When I attended high school one of my closest friends committed suicide because of some troubled spots in his life. Will and I belonged to a church which considered it a sin to be a sexually-active, exploring, gay teenager. People from our church, including me and his family, prayed God would deliver him from his 'condition' called homosexuality. God never answered those prayers. I cannot help but think those failed prayers pushed him to the despair which ended with the taking of his own life. The trauma of Will's suicide haunts me to this day.

At the time of Will's death, I decided I would never again participate in any activity that challenged how God made me, or how God made any friend or family member. Period. I had spent too much of my life living in the closet, but thanks to dear friends including others writing in this book, I have grown so much in my self-awareness and knowledge of God's Word, the Bible, and have been blessed to find new freedom in Christ. For some, however, my words may come as a surprise.

During my teen years and beyond, I was part of a very conservative Christian denomination. Rather than deal with my own gayness, I felt God wanted me to hide it, hence being in the closet proved to be a reality in my life. This led to stages of very low self-esteem and depression. I was told one could not be gay and serve Jesus. While I cannot say that I regret all of my related life choices during those many years, I can now promote a freedom in God in a healthier manner.

As a gay person growing up in a conservative Christian culture, I made many choices. Some choices we make in life cause us regret, and some do not. My choices enabled me to have a wonderful family and to experience things in my life which have helped me to become the person I am now. Nevertheless, the time has come to share how much more freedom we can realize if we do not hide what we do and who we are. If we remain in the shadows with internal conflicts and bouts of depression, then we cannot fully realize our creative blossoming in other areas of our lives. I now readily join in circles of friends who celebrate our sexuality. How wonderful it is to finally find such freedom in Christ.

I am encouraged by the 'Jesus Movement' which is happening in my denomination with an increased awareness of social justice problems. From LGBTQ rights to environmental issues, such as the danger of 'big oil' pipelines going through Native American lands and waterways, we are taking notice.

When North Carolina decided not to allow separate restrooms for transgender people, our new presiding bishop who leads our entire church, world-wide, sent a strong message to NC State Officials on June 10th, 2016. He let them know most Episcopalians did not like what their legislature and governor had done. Jesus rejoiced that day.

When authorities told Native Americans the pipeline in North Dakota would go through their water supply, my own Bishop from Eau Claire, Wisconsin went to serve alongside the protesters as an act of support and solidarity. Most Episcopalians supported his engagement. More and more, I see hope for the marginalized in our society. In fact, recently our presiding bishop issued a statement to the entire church. Michael Curry summarized:

> *When we are born anew through baptism, we promise to respect the dignity of every human being. Today, transgender people and indeed the entire LGBT community need us to keep that promise. By doing so, we can bear witness to the world that Jesus has shown us another way — the way of love.*
>
> – The Episcopal Church, Public Affairs Office, June 28th, 2016

Statistics show support for our movement. Teen suicide among LGBTQ teens is dropping now that marriage equality is the law of the land. This is good news. People feel more hopeful and included.

I help build shelters for LGBTQ young people in different areas of the U.S. In the past such shelters did not exist and gay kids had an even harder time having been thrown out of their 'Christian' homes. Homelessness devastates well enough, but when you are gay, the issues posed become even tougher. We endeavor to make their situation less traumatic.

I encourage you to watch the "It Gets Better" videos on You-Tube. The message remains true. Life will get easier for you and for your LGBTQ friends.

The bullying that goes on in our schools, neighborhoods, and in society in general needs our attention more than ever. Appearance, gender-questioning, and the desire for young people to explore and understand their identity stand as essential issues to normal growing and healthy living.

The New Testament tells us Jesus came into our world to set us free. When we judge other people, Jesus tells us we are wrong. He came to set us free to be who we are and free to love all people. Unfortunately, humans still build walls, rather than welcome and celebrate others and their diversity. Much work remains to be done, but, thanks be to God, doors are flying open. Even church doors. The light of God's love and acceptance is gaining ground and is growing in power and good understanding. Bright lights are shining. More help is on the way. Extraordinary people from around the globe are speaking out, coming out, and sharing their new, convincing, and healthy understanding of human sexuality. God is at work. God's freedom will prevail. Love must prevail. The time has come.

I pray the age-old cycle of fear and hate will further subside and God's perfect love will cast out, perhaps force out, fear.

Mark S. Ricker is pastor of three Episcopal churches in Colorado: St. John's in Granby, Cranmer Chapel in Winter Park, and Trinity in Kremmling. Mark served as priest at St. Andrew's Episcopal Church in Ashland, Wisconsin from 2013-2016, where his church began free Friday night community meals.

The Divine Spark

McGregors Are Queers

by Anonymous

Someone chalked 'McGregors are Queers' on our driveway. I was 14. Summer of 1969. I can still feel the disgust of my father scuffing out the word 'queers' while he spat 'do you know what that means?'

I knew full well what it meant. That word was me and I was being scuffed out. That part of me could never be. Never see the light of day. But that THAT WAS indeed all there was of ME.

As a teenager, without my sexuality, little else existed. I could concentrate on nothing without my sexuality screaming at me. Raging hormones and budding awareness of sexual attraction are endemic to being a teenager. Having to hide sexual attraction is an almost insurmountable task. Sexuality permeates everything a teen-ager does and thinks, 24/7. But I, and everyone else, hated mine. It remained hidden, not allowed, and therefore so much larger within me.

When necessary, along with everyone else, I laughed and insulted people who seemed to fit my feelings so others wouldn't suspect me. And as I vilified others, I knew the scorn could easily be directed at me.

It's particularly insidious when what is hated isn't obvious. The people with power invited me to participate in hate for myself. For self-preservation, I did. At least if the hate were directed at short people or fat people or native Americans or black people or people with Southern accents or Semitic people or people with an obvious difference, the subjects would not be expected to participate in the slander. The haters might actually wait until the hated were not within earshot to spew their vitriol.

The writer chooses to remain anonymous. The surname "McGregor" is a pseudonym.

Freak Out to Peace Out

by Katie Makolondra

Life as a teenager in an ultra-conservative part of Wisconsin was the worst. To begin with, I had non-traditional parents. My mom had a physical disability and I viewed my dad as an elderly man because he was twenty years her senior. They were nonconformists and political philosophers. The one good thing was we attended the "hippie" church in town that housed a brilliant, liberal pastor who preached the values of being human. He did not spew any controlling, literal interpretations of the Bible. We had no fire and brimstone at Hope United Church of Christ, only good feelings and a strong, supportive community. Our church, however, was in the city of Sturgeon Bay, far from the boondocks of my school district's boundaries.

All my classmates were religious. This is not hyperbole. The kids in my class were either strict Catholics or the kind of Lutheran where men sit on one side of the aisle and the women on the other, all in silent reverie of the pastor's threats of eternal damnation. I did not fit in at all.

I recall my first experience at my best friend's church one Sunday morning. She warned me it would be boring, but made consolation promises of Schwann's ice cream sundaes afterward. The sermon dwelled on David and Goliath and burning in Hell. Every time the pastor mentioned, almost casually, burning in Hell, he looked right at me. I have seldom felt as hated as I did that morning. It penetrated my heart. At that moment I convinced myself he knew I was weird. And by weird, I mean queer.

The slow realization I was a lesbian sunk in like molasses in winter. In first grade whenever Nora came near I had my first collection of butterflies fluttering in my stomach. She and I would play married couple, complete with kisses and cuddles. It seemed innocent enough to the outside, I am sure, but for me I knew our "friendship" wasn't normal.

At nine or ten years old, while watching a horror movie, I asked my mom if it were possible for me to have a crush on girls. I remember getting red in the face and a little sick to my stomach just asking such a shameful question. She laughed at me and assured me I liked boys and I definitely did not like girls that way. I begrudgingly accepted her opinion, but it didn't sit right. My attraction to beautiful women was strong.

As I got older I had crushes on all my best friends with increasing intensity. I became obsessed with Tiffany; simply had to have sleepovers at Jamie's house; and don't get me started on Julie.

Yet I knew enough to establish public crushes on boys to avoid becoming the target of a witch hunt. I always had an overarching sense that being gay out loud would endanger me. I would get bullied relentlessly and possibly attacked. Actual gay bashing truly existed where I came from and the idea of getting caught, then ostracized and injured, terrified me.

Nevertheless, one can hide the truth for only so long. In seventh grade, I developed the strongest feelings I had ever known. Actual love. Jodie stood out as a funky, oppositional rule-breaker.

She was not a girlie girl. She was crass, she smoked menthols, and she had a boy haircut. Jodie was perfect. After swimming at her cottage, I will never forget as we showered in our swimsuits to get the lake off our skin. I felt compelled to wash her hair. I desired intimacy and actually went for it without thinking.

As I started massaging shampoo into her hair, she looked at me – and 'looked' is not the right word. She knew me with her eyes. Her smile faded. She pushed me away and got out of the shower still full of shampoo.

Jodie had me call my mom to come pick me up. She stopped answering my phone calls and threw the notes I had passed to her in the trash. Worse yet, Jodie told people.

I had already served as a target for bullying because of my unusual, non-local family, and my individuality. I always prayed – literally prayed – nobody would figure me out. But now kids started teasing me, calling me dyke, laughing in my face… and this was the only interaction I received. Nobody wanted to have sleepovers. Nobody wanted to hang out. I was the loneliest I had ever been. My once-friend's mom called me a "fat dykey hoe" to my other friends at an awards ceremony.

No tears could fall fast enough from the amount of pain I suffered. I began cutting myself and started smoking. Eventually I fell into a group of misfits who self-medicated their quirks away.

Thankfully, my own church, my sanctuary away from the emotional suffering as a queer teenager, became the first church in our region to openly accept gay members. I remember the day like yesterday. The gay and lesbian congregation members put rainbow stickers on their name tags and we hung rainbow flags around the inner worship area. I swallowed everything and memorized the faces and names of the queer members of my church. These people always existed. I had never known they were LGBT. If I could have known sooner, I would have had an outlet for all the confusion and frustration. Maybe I could have shown more bravery. Yet, this one gesture by Hope Church actually gave me hope. I realized maybe someday I could live as openly gay. Could someday hurry up?

In high school my friend Amy, who knew nothing of my sexual orientation, took me in during hard times. She went to my church. I felt certain I could tell her my secret without repercussion. After a night of liquid courage, I asked her if I could tell her something. I was sick to my stomach from nerves, but felt confident she would be throwing rainbow confetti and celebrating my coming out. Wrong.

I told her I was "bi," not even true, but it felt safer than straight-up lesbian. Amy left the room. She would not let me sleep in her room anymore and preferred I find an entirely different living situation. My heart dropped to the floor. I couldn't stand the rejection. I felt betrayed by my own self. How could I have let my guard down? Didn't I know better than to trust anyone? Amy finally did come around, but our friendship had changed forever.

The accumulation of false starts and failures pushed me deep into the closet. I decided I would call my endless longing for female companionship a horrible fetish, if not a curse. I tried to ignore my nature. At college, I dated a few women, all disasters, and therefore sought a different type of relationship. I met my now ex-husband and hunkered down internally for a life of regret and sacrifice for the greater good of fitting into society.

We had three children, built a wonderful life together, and enjoyed a legitimate friendship. A friendship I could no longer keep as I got older.

I turned thirty and went to Minneapolis with my best friend for a night of dancing and cutting loose. We ended up at the Gay 90s, an awesome LGBT nightclub, where I locked eyes with a foxy, butch lesbian. We danced all night.

When I woke the next day I told my friend I was totally a lesbian. "What do I do? I have a husband. I have kids! Should I keep waiting it out until the baby is eighteen?" We strategized and planned.

I went home to a very honest and painful conversation with my husband. We began to detach emotionally from one another and started the process to end our marriage.

Without Messiah Lutheran I could never have legitimatized my identity as a lesbian. I joined the church to help ease my mind about the monotony and misery of marriage by focusing on the other joys of life and on God's ultimate plan. I am a firm believer in God and find solace in His ways, but I particularly needed the moral compass delivered by Pastor Nancy's sermons. Pastor Nancy accepted my struggles and guided me through the most difficult times. I thought my love for my husband served me well enough to carry me through life. He remained a dear, dear friend, but I felt no passion. The touch of a man made me feel violated. I was stuck and Pastor Nancy helped me come to accept the path laid out for me by God.

I was never an abomination, as my former community believed. I was a child of God. My place in His eyes did not change as a lesbian.

I am now happily married to my wife Kate. She is full of piss and vinegar, love and empathy, and she makes my children feel adored. I have never felt love like this in all my life.

I am out and stay fairly vocal about it. I work in a middle school and want any other questioning students not to suffer as I did. I want to serve as an advocate and a mentor. Though the past remains dark and sad for me, the present and future look perfect. I am so grateful to have faith and to receive support in my faith here in the north woods. No more suffering in the heartland.

Katie Makolondra and her partner were happily married in December 2016 at Messiah Lutheran Church, Washburn, Wisconsin.
Currently working at Bayfield Public School, Katie is in the process of getting her bachelor's degree in Special Education.

Love Conquers All

by Mary Bondeson

One of my favorite memories as a mom is my son coming out to me. He had been having a classmate come over after school, and it became obvious to me they wanted to be together. Yet, I was still surprised when he stood before me, shifting from one foot to the other, hands jammed into his jeans pockets and said, "Mom, I've been wanting to tell you something for awhile, I'm just gonna come out and say it: I'm bisexual!"

"Oh, I thought you were going to tell me you're gay!"

No less than four months earlier, I offered a familiar refrain that I often tucked into our heart-to-heart conversations about relationships and life plans: "You never know, you might be gay. And that would be ok."

He countered: "Mom, I'm pretty sure I'm not gay!"

Growing up, my son had free reign in our household to play with clothes, hair, persona, hero roles, heroine roles, you name it. I figured why shouldn't a boy have as much fun being as expressive as girls? His older sister took great delight in dressing him up in her now-too-small fancy clothes and jewelry. They had a treasure chest filled with colorful fabric, all manner of skirts and dresses, capes, high heels, masks, wands, fairy wings, hats, make-up. While my daughter had fun with perms and braiding hair, my son would use glitter glue to make outrageous mohawks in neon green or blue. A favorite memory is seeing him layer a dress over another dress, a skirt on his head which he swished this way and that as though he had long hair, several layers of bling around his neck, and high heels. Sword in hand, he would race up the slide bottom to top, then leap in one bound from the upper platform to the ground. He was a stealthy ninja flying around the yard in a fantasyland of his own creation; in other words, he was being a healthy fun-loving kid.

These escapades did not go unnoticed by others who were not as comfortable as I was with not labeling how my children played. A sister queried if it was "normal." My husband squirmed to find out his son wore a dress to a community dance. Our day care center prohibited him from wearing skirts or dresses "to make sure he didn't get teased." I never stewed over the relationship between creative play and sexual identity/orientation. We could hire researchers to study this, but really, who cares? I'm sure they would find that of the many children who engage in creative dress-up which blurs the gender "line" (it's not really a line, but that's another tangent), some are gay, some are bi, some are transgender, some are straight, and some don't even care to designate.

Negotiating situations that came with his first boyfriend presented some difficult challenges. His boyfriend was not ready to come out to his parents, knowing that their strong Christian upbringing was at odds with his sexual orientation. We had many conversations about privacy, secrecy, and confidentiality. I took an oath not to share this new information with anyone, knowing that in a small community, if my friends knew my son was gay, that news would soon spread. I felt robbed of a rite of passage enjoyed by every mother of a teenager: sharing the joy of your child's first romance. Instead of excited phone calls, facebook posts, and fun chats during soccer games, I was counseling two boys to be careful and never get caught holding hands in public, much less share a kiss.

I had always welcomed into my home everyone whom my children cared about. If they were friends and they behaved in respectful ways, they were part of our family. Our place became the safe place for my son's gay friends. As many of them came to know me, they would confide some of their personal struggles and family conflicts. It was painful to know that many of these teenagers did not have unconditional acceptance at home. Revealing their sexual orientation came with the risk of being rejected, or not having a place to live. Their uncertainty and self-doubt created a very palpable vulnerability.

This story has a happy ending, however. Or, more accurately, my son's life continues to unfold in happy, healthy ways. Within two years of coming out to me, he forgot I was still living under the vow of secrecy: "Mom, I've been out at school for a long time now!" His school administrators protected and supported him. His first boyfriend finally gave his parents the ultimatum after his first year at college: either you stop trying to convert me or I won't be coming home any longer. They did.

My son knows himself. He digs deep to uncover his own truths. He is compassionate, caring, articulate, interested in life, adventurous, excited to learn and grow.

In preparing this story I asked my son to share his thoughts. The following statements are paraphrased.

My parents were liberal and I knew they were progressive in their views about gays; I had gay family members who were loved and included. Still, it was an act of courage for me to come out. It doesn't make sense. It's not logical to say I knew it would be okay AND it was difficult to do, but it was. I was nervous and anxious. Maybe because I had experiences as a kid where I was shut down for how I expressed myself. It took me several years to come to terms with my sexuality. As early as six years old I was curious about being with both girls and boys. I knew this was not the norm. I felt like it was wrong even though it was natural for me.

I carried this internal conflict all through my coming-of-age years. I pushed this away for a long time. Not until I had the experience of being with a boy and being intimate did I know if this was right for me. Likewise, I needed to explore being with girls to eventually understand that although I appreciated girls, my so-called attraction was more a desperate attempt to lessen the burden of my true identity; to make it seem I had some aspect of normalcy, like I was half normal instead of being straight up gay.

Homosexuality in our society is stereotyped as just a sexual issue. But it's so much more than that. It is intimacy, connecting with another human being, sharing yourself, being included socially, doing fun things together, introducing new people and new things to each other. Regardless of your gender attraction for intimacy, there remains the mysterious miracle of two people touching souls.

For those who struggle with accepting the gender revolution that seems to be sweeping our world, I would offer some tidbits to encourage open-mindedness:

1) Educate yourself.

Read people's stories, find out about new language used to describe gender identity and orientation. Explore resources. Some of my favorite websites are:

www.glsen.org

Gay Lesbian Straight Education Network is a powerhouse of information regarding teen issues surrounding all forms of sexual identity and orientation, with comprehensive resources for schools, teachers, and students.

www.pflag.org

Parents and Friends of Lesbians and Gays also includes transgender people and the rainbow of expressions and orientations that are blossoming in our culture right now. Find a local chapter near you and attend meetings. There is no substitute for face-to-face dialogue and you will meet some of the nicest, most caring people on the planet.

www.itspronouncedmetrosexual.com

This very creative and engaging site was started by a former stand-up comic who created the "genderbread person," a light-hearted but thorough look at all things gender, with excellent links to other related sites.

2) Start talking.

Speak with friends, family, and community. Ask questions. Listen. Withhold judgement. Mull over new ideas. Ask more questions. Turn to love. Repeat.

3) Let nothing interfere with your love.

Jesus and the Beatles were right.

The evening my son came out to me was followed by a long, full talk about his new boyfriend and how he was going to negotiate situations with school, friends, and family. He took charge by insisting on controlling his coming-out process. He considered how his news would affect different family members and made thoughtful choices about how to introduce (or not introduce) his new boyfriend. He was fifteen. The joy I felt that he would share this with me was so great I immediately popped to my feet and gave him a huge, teary-eyed hug. After several hours of conversation he said, "Mom, could we possibly not talk about this for, like, at least two weeks?"

I don't have a gay son. I have a loving, caring, compassionate, intelligent, engaging and thoughtful son who happens to be gay. I couldn't be more proud.

Mary Bondeson lived in Washburn, Wisconsin for 34 years with her two children and husband John Mydels, where they founded and ran the Friends of the Earth Garden Center and the Harmony School of Music. Mary now lives and works in Door County, Wisconsin where she teaches choral music at Gibraltar Secondary School.

Grace Upon Grace

by Rev. Dale Chesley

I was raised a Lutheran; but more in the tradition which defined a Christian by what I did not do, than how I lived through Christ. A Christian doesn't smoke, drink alcohol, do drugs, take God's name in vain, or have sex outside of marriage; a few among the plethora of 'don'ts.' The same Lutheran tradition viewed the Bible as a sacred book that gave us a mandatory and absolute guide for our lives. If a person wanted "salvation," then one received Jesus as Lord and Savior and followed the rules. As a result, faith became something which demanded my responsibility, and God stood as the One to whom I remained responsible.

Such standards about right and wrong loomed large. I had to live the right life and avoid all sins which brought judgment upon me. Sexual sins sat at the top of every list. Dealing with my own sexuality ate at my conscience, and when the church taught me the abomination of homosexuality, it came as a relief in certain ways because I was not homosexual. At least I got that one right. I sinned elsewhere, plenty, but the one about not becoming a homosexual came easy. I did not understand homosexuality and had little incentive to try, because here we had one sin I did not struggle with. I learned homosexuality represented a sin, a Biblical standard, no arguing about it.

Another Biblical standard taught me to reject the idea women could serve as pastors. The tradition of our church had no room for it because the Bible taught it was wrong. But as part of the American Lutheran Church, we eventually voted to ordain women, and that confused me. Nevertheless, I remained faithful to my teachings.

When I attended seminary, the sins initially taught to me were challenged in a number of ways. It made me look at women in ministry differently. I also learned new things about what the Bible says.

I remember back in my confirmation classes a surprising word caught my attention. In Luther's meaning of the second commandment, "You shall not take the name of the Lord your God in vain." Luther tells us to not use God's name superstitiously. How might one do that? The best I could come up with was the ways in which we used God's name like a good luck charm. For example, if a person crosses themselves before shooting a free throw in a basketball game, thinking God would then help them make the basket, that felt a bit superstitious to me. Superstitions almost always have their roots in fear. As I studied at seminary, I started to see how often I looked at the Bible superstitiously, out of fear, instead of love.

In 1 Timothy we read these words:

Let a woman learn in silence with full submission. I permit no woman to teach or to have authority over a man; she is to keep silent. For Adam was formed first, then Eve; and Adam was not deceived, but the woman was deceived and became a transgressor. Yet she will be saved through childbearing, provided they continue in faith and love and holiness, with modesty.

— 1 Timothy 2: 11-15 NRSV

That kind of settled the issue of ordaining women as pastors. But it also ignored completely Galatians 3:28:

There is no longer Jew or Greek, there is no longer slave or free, there is no longer male and female, for all of you are one in Christ Jesus.

Suddenly I realized the faith I grew up with had no good way of dealing with contradictions in the Bible. In fact, it denied any contradictions existed. The word 'superstitious' took on a new meaning. If we bring to the Bible confessions of believing it presents one unified understanding of God without cultural influence, then we approach Scripture with a closed mind rather than an open heart.

When in seminary, I met three women in my formulation of faith group. I watched them. I listened to them. I witnessed the embodiment of Galatians 3:28. Obviously the women differed from me physically, but in intellect, in sense of call, in gifts for ministry, in love for Christ, in sense of humor, in passion for the Gospel, I saw no differences aside from our individuality. I recognized some would make better pastors than I would. It was not my place to deny the work of God in them.

Besides, I have never believed for a second that women would be saved through childbearing. I have always believed they would be saved the same way I am saved, through the grace of God, because of the cross and the resurrection of Jesus Christ.

In spite of some superstitious discomfort from my old way of understanding things, I found myself joyfully and confidently embracing the decision of our National Church to ordain women.

Change often comes slowly. Even though I began to believe our church should ordain women, I continued to believe homosexuality amounted to sin and disqualified such people from ordained ministry. But an example had been set and I believe the Spirit of God was at work in me.

I don't know if Tony Campolo was the first to say it, but he said Jesus would never say, "Love the sinner, hate the sin." I have heard many people say the same about gay people. On the other hand, he also suggested Jesus would say, "Love the sinner, hate your own sin." I ask myself, what does it mean to hate my own sin? I have come to believe it means I don't have time to focus on the sins of others. I have all I can handle to hate my own sin. I had to ask how such a view would guide me in my understanding of homosexuality from a believer's standpoint.

Again, I had to look at Scripture and question whether I had rooted my search in superstition. Romans 1 contains text about men and women who stick their fist in the face of God by denying their natural sexuality in order to seek sexual relations with members of the same sex. Such a passage does not describe a young teenager struggling with his or her desire for a person of the same sex. They are not rebelling against God. They simply realize they are wired differently and are trying to cope with what it means in a society filled with so much condemnation, a society which hates others' sins.

As I have listened to the voices of homosexuals, I hear them saying they made no choice in the matter. It is the way they are born and they are living out what is natural for them. Then I hear heterosexual people claim it is a choice. Yet it makes most sense to listen to those who live through the experience, rather than claiming to defend an ideal which often originates from their own decision on how to interpret the Bible.

As I have tried to figure out what I believe, given my history, the Bible remains at the vital center of my convictions. Time after time, as I ask what Jesus might say about homosexuality, a scripture comes to mind. Since Jesus says nothing about it, we need to listen to other things he said. I had no desire to change my mind about homosexuality simply because it became the current trend in society.

The scripture Matthew 21:28-32 kept occurring to me. Speaking to religious leaders Jesus says, "What do you think? A man had two sons; he went to the first and said, 'Son, go and work in the vineyard today.' He answered, 'I will not;' but later he changed his mind and went. The father went to the second and said the same; and he answered, 'I go, sir'; but he did not go. Which of the two did the will of his father?" They said, "The first." Jesus said to them, "Truly I tell you, the tax collectors and the prostitutes are going into the kingdom of God ahead of you. For John the Baptist came to you in the way of righteousness and you did not believe him, but the tax collectors and the prostitutes believe him; and even after you saw it, you did not change your minds and believe him."

Jesus said the people the religious leaders considered sinners, people on the fringes of society, would go into the kingdom ahead of them. From a young age this has greatly offended me. I could not understand the message from Jesus because I considered myself one of the religious ones. As I have come to understand the ways of Jesus, it makes sense. He always has a heart for those whom everyone else would condemn.

When I asked the question of who comprises those people today, given the context of the opinion of many religious leaders today, I understood homosexual people fall into the category of those fringe people. Many church people today, who hate other peoples' sin rather than their own, point fingers, exclude, and draw the circle of grace in such a way as to leave gay people out.

I have come to believe Jesus wants me to love the ones on the fringe in the same way; to recognize they go into the kingdom of God ahead of me should I point my finger at them, instead of hating my own sin. I have become cognizant anytime I draw the circle of grace in such a way that if it leaves anyone out, Jesus will stand outside the circle with them.

The question of whether homosexual activity constitutes a sin I must leave in God's hands. It is clear to me it does not constitute a sin to be homosexual. It is also clear to me I am guilty of all sorts of actions I believe are sinful. I have to focus on my own sins for which I seek the grace of God. Likewise for homosexual people. If God does not condemn their committed, loving relationships, then I will stay out of it. I have enough to worry about with my own sin.

In some ways I remain captive to the superstitious ways of my past which I must deal with all the time. I now acknowledge I possess no qualifications to name other people's sins. I can see the Bible does not speak with as much clarity concerning homosexuality as some would claim. God has moved my heart to yield to God's love. I have gay friends who lack nothing in spiritual gifts compared to straight friends. I have gay pastor friends who have proved themselves effective, loving spiritual leaders in Christ's Church. They are called in the same way I am called. They live as redeemed sinners, no differently than my life as a redeemed sinner. God makes use of them in the same ways God makes use of me.

I sit today with open arms to those who are gay and also want to do ministry. I see them as whole people in the faith since all of us remain broken in some way.

It is not an easy thing to examine how hate and love find their place in the life of the Church. I hold the opinion the righteous cannot rise to the level of "hating the sin but loving the sinner," as many would have it. But I also believe the sincerity of the sentiment and those who say such things often speak from the center of their hearts. They seek faithfulness to God and to what they believe God wants. Yet I also believe many remain captive to a superstitious way of understanding the Bible and thus find it impossible to consider God might call to God's flock someone they believe the Bible labels sinful. I say this not to justify such actions, but to observe more love emanates from them than often gets received. Loving, faithful people whose self-righteousness means they shun homosexual people have hearts which want good things for gay people. They strive for faithfulness to God, but like all of us, they live as saints and sinners at the same time.

Nonetheless, such heartfelt convictions still hurt gay people, the hatred admittedly scathing at times. Hatred in the name of love is still hatred, a great failing of the church I love. I confess it as our sin.

For me, the example of Jesus loving those on the fringes compels me to do likewise. I invite them, in Jesus's name, to the center of the circle of grace. I am one also invited and Jesus is the host. Our circle stands as a place of holy fellowship. I welcome as I have been welcomed. Christ loves all of us, together, and we offer that love back in the way we care for his body; in the way we care for each other.

Pastor Dale Chesley is in his 39th year of ministry. Married with two grown daughters, Dale serves as pastor at Good Shepherd Lutheran Church in Ashland, Wisconsin.

The Divine Spark

God's Justice, God's Love

by Rev. Nate Aaseng

Those who believe the Bible condemns same-sex relationships subscribe to a Sacred Writ view of biblical authority. Sacred Writ believes the Bible itself represents something close to divine, that it says exactly what God wants it to say, and nothing more, in exactly the words God wanted it said.

If you truly believe such a point of view, however, then you cannot pick and choose which parts of the Bible you accept and don't accept. If you believe God condemns homosexuality because of selected verses, then you also must believe it an abomination to:

- eat pork; Leviticus 11:7-8
- eat shrimp, clams, oysters, scallops, crab, lobster, and squid; Leviticus 11:10-12
- do any work on the Sabbath, under penalty of death; Exodus 35:2
- let your furnace run on the Sabbath, even when it's -20 degrees outside; Exodus 35:3
- wear any clothing made of blended material; Deuteronomy 22:11

- shave or trim your beard or have a tattoo; Leviticus 19:27-28

- be a woman and wear pants. Deuteronomy 22:5

Furthermore, if you believe God condemns homosexuality in the Bible because of selected verses, then you must believe these with equal conviction:

- More than simply condoning slavery, God says beating a slave to death comprises righteous behavior so long as the slave survives a day or two. Exodus 21:20-21

- Polygamy violates no law of God – the patriarch Jacob had four wives.

- God not only tolerates genocide but sometimes demands it. Joshua 8:24-27, 10:40

- A defiant child must be stoned to death. Deuteronomy 21:18-21

- God requires you to sell all you have and give the money to the poor – you do not have a choice. Luke 18:18-22

- No one who is lame or has a visible defect can become a pastor and no one who has a blemish can approach the altar for communion. Leviticus 21:18-21

- It is shameful for a woman to read a lesson or say a prayer in church. I Corinthians 14:34-35

- Acceptable behavior includes offering your daughters to a mob to be gang raped. Genesis 19:8

When people complain that denominations such as the Evangelical Lutheran Church of America (ELCA) is no longer a Bible-based church, they mean the ELCA is not a Sacred Writ church. It never has been. ELCA follows the teachings of Martin Luther, who urged people to read the Bible in light of its central claims of who God is and how God relates to people.

If one reads the Bible in light of the central claims of what God embodies and how God relates to people, the Bible tells a very different story than what critics believe.

Look at biblical texts central to faith from a law perspective:

1) In Exodus 20 we find the Ten Commandments. The issue of same-gender relationships does not appear.

2) In Matthew 22:36-40 Jesus is asked to name the essence of the law. He answers, "Love God and your neighbor." Again, homosexuality has nothing to do with it.

3) Galatians 5:14 contains a similar essence of the law. Homosexuality remains a non-factor.

4) Jesus never spoke one word about homosexuality.

Given all the above, as a matter of Jesus's commands, a Christian cannot consider committed, same-gender relationships as central to the message of the Bible.

On the other hand, Exodus 22:21-24 holds high the issue of justice for the poor, the oppressed, and the stranger. This focus occurs so often in the Bible one must consider it a principal message.

In Luke 16:19-31 failure to do justice amounts to the only sin that got the rich man sent to hell. Again, the meaning of the story remains clear — justice rides paramount.

In Matthew 25: 31-46 injustice encompasses the sin that sends people into damnation.

In Matthew 18: 23-35 someone owes the equivalent of hundreds of billions of dollars. God forgives it all. God forgives everything in this story except injustice.

The Bible states over and over that God always stands on the side of the oppressed, the downtrodden, the powerless. Given the extremely high suicide rate of LGBTQ youth and their exposure to relentless ridicule, hatred, and discrimination, who gets more oppressed than they?

How do we determine whether same-sex relationships present as a law issue (though the Bible says not an important one), or as a justice issue?

For guidance, we can rely only on our experience with God's creation. If, in one's experience, those in committed, same-gender relationships actively recruit, corrupt, and threaten the stability of the family and culture, then we face a law issue.

If, in one's experience, they are simply people who happen to be wired differently, then we face a non-issue.

If, in one's experience, they occupy a place as good friends or family, you share their pain and heartache, and feel for the abuse and persecution they experience physically and emotionally, then we confront a justice issue.

Given what the Bible says about God's absolute hatred of injustice, given Jesus's disgust with the Pharisees harping on their morality laws all the time, the Bible states unequivocally, if we should err in this matter, we had better err on the side of justice.

Pastor Nate Aaseng serves as lead pastor at St. John's Lutheran Church in Eau Claire, Wisconsin. Before pastoring, Nate worked as a research microbiologist and free-lance author of 178 published books.

The Next Step

by Aubrey Thonvold

As we honor the holiness of each person named and claimed by the Divine, it is important not to stop there. Love lasts as a powerful emotion which can transform many lives. The work of welcome, inclusion, and celebration of lesbian, gay, bisexual, transgender, queer, intersex, and asexual (LGBTQIA+) people continues throughout life, manifested through advocacy.

Faith communities have a number of options on how they can live a lifelong journey of supporting LGBTQIA+ people. ReconcilingWorks, a national non-profit organization, is committed to accompanying people and ministry settings through outreach, education, and support.

Ministries across the USA and Canada have an opportunity to partner with ReconcilingWorks to join a national coalition of Reconciling in Christ (RIC) communities. This coalition consists of synods, congregations, seminaries, campus ministries, and Bible camp ministries who have approved a public welcome statement of all sexual orientations and gender identities. These congregations live out their welcome in unique and evolving ways to meet the needs of their communities and the people they serve. Their work endures as life giving and life saving for LGBTQIA+ people. The power of being named, seen, and cared for can transform lives. To read such welcome statements, watch video vignettes of the diversity of congregations, and to learn more about the resources available, please visit www.reconcilingworks.org.

Working side by side for justice and equity for others, we can reclaim the power of scripture. We can use it to bring healing, wholeness, and liberation for a community of people historically told they count for less based upon stagnant scriptural interpretation and manipulation of authority.

For those who are LGBTQIA+, live boldly in the truth you are fearfully and wonderfully made. Without you living as the beloved person you are, this world would not survive. As a queer person myself, I need you to show up and walk alongside me so I can live as my best self, knowing I remain whole, valued, and loved.

For those of you who join as allies, ask members of the LGBTQIA+ community what we need from you. Trust us to know what works best for ourselves.

If you define yourself as someone living with questions, then continue to seek understanding and remain open to what you may learn and receive.

We can only accomplish our holy work when we are in relationship to the Divine and to one another. May our hearts and minds stay open to performing beyond the "Golden Rule" of "treating others as you want others to treat you." Let us aim for the "Platinum Rule" of "treating others as they would want to be treated."

Aubrey Thonvold is the Executive Director of ReconcilingWorks, based in St. Paul, Minnesota. The publisher of this book, Messiah Lutheran Church, Washburn, Wisconsin, is an RIC congregation.

Epilogue

by Rev. Nancy Hanson

Of the nearly 7.2 billion people on earth, about 2.2 billion call themselves Christian. Those who follow the teachings of Jesus include a very diverse group. Each sect undertakes the examination, interpretation, and application of their ancient texts, the most popular of which remains the Bible. The world's other religions comprise approximately 4 billion people. The approximately one billion people who classify as secular, nonreligious, agnostic, and atheist include a great many who consider themselves "spiritual, but not religious."

Pointedly, many of us feel some kind of spiritual tug. We want something more. We hope for an afterlife however defined. Faced with any number of sets of beliefs, we often choose someone or something to follow. In my case, largely due to my upbringing, I subscribe to Christianity. Most followers of Jesus know of His care for people on the margins.

If I am thirsty, hungry, naked, sick, a stranger, or if I am in prison, Christians are encouraged to see the face of Christ in me. LGBTQ people, however, remain the only marginalized group who get clobbered by the Bible. Living on the margins of society already has difficult challenges. If I am poor and you use the Bible to justify walking alongside me, then I may be touched by the Jesus in your Bible. But if I am a person who is LGBTQ and you use your Bible to tell me my same-gender attraction or my desire to dress a particular way constitutes wrongfulness and sin, then what course do I have? I have to wonder about God. I have little choice but to forsake whatever such a God has to offer.

A piano teacher, a medical doctor, my cousin Chuck, deep within me I knew them only as people, nothing more, just souls trying to get from one life to the next. I often wonder, "What would it feel like to be told your natural sexual desire is sinful? An abomination? What would it feel like to be told by the most minted religious people and all their followers that I am inherently disordered?"

As a straight person not once have I heard such comments directed at me. From my first crush, I have lived within the privilege of the majority. When we become infatuated, fall in love, get engaged, married, our society views us as normal. If I am LGBTQ, however, every single step of the way in sexual attraction becomes riddled with, "What do they think of me? Do they like gay people? Can I hold hands? I'm attracted, but how can I know if this person will like me back?" Admittedly, straight people experience the latter, but without the other concerns. I am indeed a privileged heterosexual.

Having a minority sexual orientation presents many unique difficulties. One of them is that millions of "religious" people believe they know for an absolute certainty that who you are does not fit into God's plan. I cannot fathom a more wrongful teaching.

Hence, the push behind this book. Of all humanity's pie, the slice here consists of pretty much Christian and Lutheran. Even if you fall into the nonreligious category, please take the time to read and understand because we need to spread the message. If we help one person move from thoughts like: "I'm a screw up. I must be evil. Who I am does not fit. I am a freak," to thoughts like: "I am a beloved child of God who made me and loves me just as I am," then we will make our world a better, safer, and more peaceful place.

Let's do it.

Love in Christ,

Nancy Hanson

The Divine Spark

Acknowledgments

by Rev. Nancy Hanson

I acknowledge all those whose divine sparks have been shining in my life since the start of this book project. Members of First Lutheran and Messiah Lutheran Churches have supported both my sabbatical and the creation of this book. They have encouraged me to disseminate copies during my travels. The book would not have been possible without them. It is an honor and joy to serve these two flocks. So many times they have shepherded me instead of the other way around. I am grateful.

God's divine spark resides in everyone. The body of Christ has many members and each member has a unique gift. A toe, a leg, a kidney, a knee bone - each part of the body has its function. We do not all have the same gifts. Editor Philip Sorensen brought an attentive spark to the project reviewing every word with his red pen. Mark Babel and Will Pipkin, owners of Copy That, adopted the book as their own. They gave the utmost in time and talent with design of the book – interior and cover – and important help with the title, content, and production.

Martha Shultz, an account executive at Smartpress, handled the printing of this book with prompt professionalism.

Thank you to Bishop Yvette Flunder who has given us permission to print part of Article One on the cover as well as the entire Christians United statement on page 105.

Without external funding, I would not be going on sabbatical. Without the sabbatical preparation, the idea to compile this book might not have happened. Tremendous gratitude goes to the Lilly Endowment National Clergy Renewal Program for believing in this project and paying for most of the sabbatical expenses.

Pastor Donna Duensing, the spouse of one of my favorite seminary teachers, gave me numerous tips to enhance my upcoming trip to Patmos, Greece. Donna introduced me to Villy Tsakona through whom I met Costas Canakis, both university professors in Greece whose assistance has exceeded my expectations. Villy translated a few of the stories into Greek which you can find on the blog sabbatical2018.blogspot.com. Costas has agreed to help me connect with students at the University of the Aegean. I am touched by their kindness.

My friends and family are too numerous to mention by name. You know who you are and I am so thankful for you.

Lastly, I am thankful for my husband Robert who introduced me to the Orthodox Church. He is loved and nurtured by God through his faith. I look forward to learning how Orthodox Christians in Greece embrace cross-generational faith formation, sexual orientation, and gender identities. Join me in praying for an open heart as we continue to find the divine spark in everyone.

Thank you, all.

Nancy Hanson
February, 2018

Resources

Publications

Queer Virtue: What LGBTQ People Know About Life and Love and How It Can Revitalize Christianity, by Rev. Elizabeth M. Edman

A Brief Guide to Ministry with LGBTQIA Youth, by Cody J. Sanders

Wrestling with God and Men: Homosexuality and the Jewish Tradition, by Steven Greenburg

Queer Clergy: A History of Gay and Lesbian Ministry in American Protestantism, by R. W. Holmen

Emergency Mental Health Providers

Trevor Lifeline – 866-488-7386
Trained counselors are available 24/7 for those who are in crisis or anyone in need of a safe and judgment-free place to talk.

Lifeline – 800-273-8255
Your confidential and toll free call goes to the nearest crisis center in the Lifeline national network. mentalhealth.gov

The Divine Spark

About the Sabbatical

Excerpts of "Forming Lifelong Faith in a Loving God" sabbatical proposal from Messiah Lutheran and First Lutheran Churches on behalf of Rev. Nancy Hanson

Pastor Nancy Hanson grew up within an environment of love and acceptance by family, by church members of all ages, and by God. Nancy's parents upheld Christian practices of weekly worship and education, home devotions, and service. Nancy recognizes the value of having inherited such faith in a loving God. She compares her experience with that of her cousin Chuck who lived on a farm about one mile from Nancy's farm. Chuck grew up with faith in God and frequent church attendance. But when he realized he was gay, he felt shame and assumed he was condemned by God. He internalized a home, cultural, and church message of homosexuality as an unacceptable sin. He died an early death at the age of 32.

Nancy answered the call to ordained ministry as a second career principally because she wanted to articulate God's abundant love to those who have received messages of condemnation, such as: God hates fags; love the sinner, hate the sin. Nancy obtained her grounding at Pacific Lutheran Theological Seminary (PLTS) in Berkeley, California, acquiring a theology which views people with a variety of sexual orientations and gender identities as equally loved by God.

The sabbatical project, *Forming Lifelong Faith in a Loving God*, connects Pastor Nancy with her two congregations raising awareness of how one forms a lifelong faith in a loving God. During the sabbatical Nancy will focus on:

a) learning how churches support cross-generational faith formation within the church and at home;

b) learning how churches support LGBTQ people; and

c) discovering ways church people of all ages, sexual orientation, and gender identities can help each other form faith in a loving God.

During her sabbatical Nancy will observe the extent to which church people and non-church people in both the U.S. and Greece address cross-generational faith formation and LGBTQ inclusion.

Members and friends of Messiah and First have written stories for a book called *The Divine Spark*. Nancy will distribute the book while on sabbatical, enabling Nancy's parishoners to share their journeys of LGBTQ inclusion. Progressive American Christians often discuss their LGBTQ identity more openly than Greek Orthodox leaders and parishoners. Nancy looks forward to learning more about what lies behind their views.

The lack of positive church messages regarding one's sexual orientation and gender identity comprises one reason why anxiety, depression, addiction, isolation, bullying, and suicide remain higher among the LGBTQ community. We want church people of all ages to learn new ways of saying:

We love you completely, as does God who accepts you, inclusive of your sexual orientation and gender identity.

Nancy Hanson, a 1979 graduate of Concordia College in Moorhead, Minnesota, received a double major in psychology and social work. She graduated from Pacific Lutheran University, Tacoma, WA in 1983 with a master's degree in counseling and guidance. Hanson worked as a church youth director and career counselor before becoming a pastor.

Books written by Nancy include: *Create Work You Love, From Pain to Joy, How to Survive and Maybe Even Thrive Your First Year of Seminary,* and *How to Survive and Maybe Even Thrive Your First Year of College.*

Nancy received her master's degree of divinity from PLTS in 2003. Initially serving a two-point parish of Bethlehem Lutheran in Newfolden, Minnesota and Nazareth Lutheran Church in Holt, Minnesota, Nancy now serves a two-point parish of Messiah Lutheran Church in Washburn, Wisconsin and First Lutheran Church in Port Wing, Wisconsin. Nancy helped start PFLAG Washburn in 2009.

The Divine Spark

Christians United Statement

Issued August 30, 2017

PREAMBLE:

As followers of Jesus Christ, we are compelled to bear witness to the love, grace, and truth of God in every generation. We believe in and serve a God who is living and active, and continually drawing us nearer to the image of Jesus Christ and the Kingdom that he proclaimed. As Christ himself assured us, following the Holy Spirit often leads us into periods of time where we are called to reflect on and reform our traditions and practices to be more clearly conformed to the mind and example of Jesus Christ. This has been the case throughout Christian history. So it is that we, like each generation before us, are called to reflect, repent, and reform our teachings and practices to be ever more closely aligned with the heart and will of God revealed to us in Jesus Christ.

In every generation there are those who resist the Spirit's leading in various ways and cling to the dogmas and traditions that God is calling us to rethink and reform. Throughout our history, those who have been on the leading edge of the Holy Spirit's sanctifying work have often found themselves initially excluded, marginalized, and demonized by some of those within established Christian institutions. In the twenty-first century, we believe that the Church finds itself once again on the brink of a new reformation, one in which the Holy Spirit is calling us to return to the Scriptures and our traditions in order to re-examine our teachings on human sexuality and gender identity.

For decades, many pastors, theologians, and reformers have boldly responded to the Holy Spirit's call and have stepped forward to call the Church to a renewed understanding of Christian teaching on sexuality and gender identity that includes, affirms, and embraces the lesbian, gay, bisexual, transgender, and non-binary, queer community as created and fully blessed by God and welcomed in to the life of the Church and society just as they are, without a need to conform to the heteronormative, patriarchal, binary sexuality and gender paradigm that Christianity has come to promote and embrace. As these prophetic voices have stepped forward, some within traditional Christian institutions have gone great lengths to demonize, exclude, and marginalize those who have faithfully followed the Holy Spirit's leading to reexamine Scripture and the tradition, claiming that these reformers were false teachers or heretics, and represented only a small percentage of Christians worldwide.

Over the past twenty years in particular, hundreds of thousands of followers of Christ around the globe have begun to respond to the prompting of the Holy Spirit and have come to understand the teachings of Scripture and our tradition to fully affirm, embrace, and celebrate the LGBT+ community and its relationships. Whilst some within the traditional Christian establishment have sought to minimize the growing wave of prominent Christian voices that have reformed their perspectives on LGBT+ inclusion, the undeniable truth remains that the so-called "traditional" Christian teaching on sexuality and gender identity is being abandoned for a more faithful, Christ-centered, and, we believe, more biblical understanding of sexuality and gender identity that magnifies the creativity of God and celebrates the wide diversity in God's creation of humanity.

A new day is dawning in the Church, and all Christians are being called to step out boldly and unapologetically in affirmation and celebration of our LGBT+ siblings as equal participants in the Kingdom of God. Therefore, in the hope of serving the Church of Jesus Christ and promoting greater reformation and reconciliation between the Church and the LGBT+ community, this coalition of Christian leaders offer the following affirmations and denials.

Article 1:

WE AFFIRM that every human being is created in the image and likeness of God and that the great diversity expressed in humanity through our wide spectrum of unique sexualities and gender identities is a perfect reflection of the magnitude of God's creative work.

WE DENY any teaching that suggests God's creative intent is limited to a gender binary or that God's desire for human romantic relationships is only to be expressed in heterosexual relationships between one man and one woman.

Article 2

WE AFFIRM that God designed marriage to be a covenantal bond between human beings who have committed to love, serve, and live a life faithfully committed to one another over the course of a lifetime.

WE DENY that God intended human romantic relationships to be limited to one man and one woman and declare that any attempts to limit the sacred or civil rights of humans to covenant and commit to love and serve one another is an affront to God's created design.

Article 3

WE AFFIRM that relationships between fallen humans have suffered great distortions resulting in various forms of infidelity and unhealthy behaviors that contribute to the suffering of humanity. We also affirm that God's desire is for all humans to enter into loving, sacrificial relationships with one another, whether romantic, platonic, or social, regardless of gender or sexual identity.

WE DENY that the fallenness of human relationships resulted in the multiplicity of sexual orientations and gender identities. Rather, fallenness manifests in the human capacity to function out of hedonistic self-interest instead of the self-giving love in whose image we are created.

Article 4

WE AFFIRM that those who are born as intersex are full and equal bearers of the image and likeness of God and are worthy of full dignity and respect. We affirm and support intersex individuals in their journey of self-realization and embracing their unique, God-created sexual orientation and gender identity, whatever it may be.

WE DENY that intersex individuals are required to conform to a gender binary or a heteronormative sexual paradigm.

Article 5

WE AFFIRM that while the male and female gender identity reflects a majority of the human family, God has created individuals whose gender identity does not fall on such a binary spectrum. We also affirm that there are many transgender individuals who are born with a physical body that is incongruent with their true gender identity, and these individuals should be supported and trusted in regards to their own self-knowledge of who they are and how God has created them.

WE DENY that forcing individuals to embrace a gender identity that matches the cultural assumptions based on their biology is a healthy practice and that the heterosexual, male/female binary is the only consistent reflection of God's holy purposes in Creation.

Article 6

WE AFFIRM that LGBT+ Christians are called to live holy and fulfilling lives that are pleasing to God through living in congruence with God's creative intent for them, and, like all Christians, are called to walk in a rhythm of life that reflects the example of Jesus Christ our Lord.

WE DENY that heterosexuality or binary gender identities are the only legitimate sexuality and gender identities that reflect the natural goodness of God's creation.

Article 7

WE AFFIRM that one may live proudly and openly as an LGBT+ individual and as a faithful follower of Jesus Christ and that LGBT+ individuals must be fully embraced and included in every level of Christian leadership, life, and ministry without exception in order for the Church to fully embrace its call to be the body of Christ. We also affirm Christ's call for the Church to be one, united in the midst of our diversity of sexual orientations, gender identities, relationships, and beliefs about the same.

WE DENY that teachings on the Biblical interpretation of sexuality and gender identity constitute a matter of orthodoxy and should be a cause for division among Christians.

Article 8

WE AFFIRM that non-inclusive teaching causes significant psychological and spiritual harm to LGBT+ individuals in Christian churches around the world. We likewise affirm that the Church of Jesus Christ is guilty of preaching a harmful message that has caused hundreds of thousands of individuals to face bullying, abuse, and exclusion from their families and communities, and must publicly repent and seek reconciliation with the LGBT+ community for the harm that has been done to them in the name of Christ.

WE DENY that any Christian who perpetuates harmful teachings and refuses to openly dialogue with LGBT+ people is living a life modeled after the faithful example of Jesus.

Article 9

WE AFFIRM that sexuality and gender identity may be expressed in a variety of different ways, including celibacy. We also affirm that commitment, consent, respect, and self-sacrificial love must be the center of any life or relationship that is to be deemed holy and upright for a Christian.

WE DENY that any individual, especially minors, should be forced to seek any form of treatment or therapy that promises to change their sexual orientation or gender identity in order to conform to a patriarchal, heteronormative model of relationship.

Article 10

WE AFFIRM that Jesus Christ has come into the world to bring salvation to all people and through his life, teachings, death, and resurrection, all are invited into redemption through Christ.

WE DENY that Christ rejects anyone from his loving embrace because of their sexuality or gender identity. We likewise deny that homosexuality, bisexuality, queer sexuality, trans identity, asexuality, or any other queer identity is sinful, distorted, or outside of God's created intent.

Christians United is an international theological statement bringing together thousands of LGBT+ affirming Christians to declare with one voice that the Church of Jesus Christ must be a place where LGBT+ people are celebrated and embraced. Christians United came as a direct response to The Nashville Statement, a document composed and signed by 150 major evangelical leaders in August 2017, which reaffirmed toxic, non-affirming theological commitments that have caused verifiable harm to countless LGBT+ people of faith around the world.

The statement was originally drafted by LGBT+ activist and theologian Brandan Robertson and was edited by a distinguished editorial board including Dr. J. R. Daniel Kirk, Bishop Joseph Tolton, Rev. Steve Chalke, and Dr. Paula Williams. In the first twenty-four hours of its release, Christians United was signed on to by over 1,000 Christians from around the world, including top theologians and the leaders of some of the world's most influential Christian denominations.

Christians United stands as a faithful witness that a new day is dawning in Christianity, a day in which the Church of Jesus Christ repents of its sin of exclusion, and swings open its doors to welcome all of God's diverse children.

More information about the statement and Christians United can be found at: www.christiansunitedstatement.org.

Christians United Statement

How to Purchase
The Divine Spark

Visit one of these independent bookstores:

Apostle Islands Booksellers
112 Rittenhouse Avenue, Bayfield, WI 54814
715-779-0200
www.ApostleIslandBooksellers.com

Chequamegon Books and Coffee
2 East Bayfield Street, Washburn, WI 54891
715-373-2899
peruse@chequamegonbooks.com
www.ChequamegonBooks.com

Spinster Books
313 Main Street West, Ashland, WI 54806
715-292-6402
www.SpinsterBooks.com

To order by mail send your name and address and $15 per book, plus shipping* to:

Messiah Lutheran Church
231 West 5th Street, Washburn, WI 54891
715-373-5378

* Shipping: $4.00 for the first book and $2.00 for each additional book, checks payable to Messiah Lutheran Church.

To pick up an order at Shepherd of the Hills Lutheran Church, 500 Blake Road South, Edina, MN, add a note to your mailed order.

Contact Messiah Lutheran for discounts on multiple copies.

Order online at www.TheSparkInMe.com, where you also can find more information about this book.

Help spread the word. Please "Like" us on Facebook.